Horse, Follow Closely

BY GAWANI PONY BOY

photographs by Gabrielle Boiselle

Horse, Follow Closely

NATIVE AMERICAN HORSEMANSHIP®

CompanionHouse Books™ is an imprint of Fox Chapel Publishers International Ltd.

Vice President—Content: Christopher Reggio

ISBN 978-1-931993-89-0

Library of Congress Cataloging-in-Publication Data
Pony Boy, GaWaNi, 1965–
    Horse, follow closely / GaWaNi Pony Boy ; photographs by Gabrielle
Boiselle.
          p. cm.
    ISBN 1-889540-22-6
    1. Indians of North America—Domestic animals. 2. Horsemanship—
    —United States. 3. Horses—Training—United States. 4. Horses—
    —United States—Folklore. I. Title.
    E98.D67P66 1998
    636.1'0835'08997—dc21   97-38660

Fox Chapel Publishing   Fox Chapel Publishers International Ltd.
903 Square Street   7 Danefield Road, Selsey (Chichester)
Mount Joy, PA 17552   West Sussex PO20 9DA, U.K.

www.facebook.com/companionhousebooks

We are always looking for talented authors. To submit an idea, please send a brief inquiry to
acquisitions@foxchapelpublishing.com.

Printed and bound in China
22   15 14 13 12 11

ACKNOWLEDGMENTS

This book is dedicated to Blaise and Riana and made possible by Creator.
—GaWaNi Pony Boy

*To my grandfather, a patient man who was well known for his ability
to talk with horses; and my father, a talented photographer.*
—Gabrielle Boiselle

Thanks to Babbit Ranches; CO Bar Ranch; Frank and Maxie Davies of Flying Heart Barn, Flagstaff, Arizona; the Howell family; K & K at Rocking Horse Stables; the Long family; the Trexler Lehigh County Game Preserve; and C & A at THE FARM. Special thanks to Ruth and Lisa, Sharon and Amy, the Assemblies Group, Inc.; and a special thank you to Gabrielle Boiselle, whose creative vision lends life to the images contained herein.
—GaWaNi Pony Boy

The time I spent with GaWaNi was very special. We could communicate with almost no words; we felt the heartbeat of nature together and enjoyed every moment of the photo shoot. Thank you GaWaNi for this experience. I would also like to extend my thanks to Andrea Morrell.
—Gabrielle Boiselle

CONTENTS

INTRODUCTION

This is the Native American horseman. For many, he represents the ultimate rider. The essence of a horseman, both his skill and intuition, goes beyond the hours he spends in the saddle.

If we are to understand our relationship with the horse, we must first understand the relationship we have with the entire animal kingdom. The human species, directly or indirectly, affects all other species on the planet, even those species we don't directly come in contact with. Every one of our actions affects all living things, and therein lies our responsibility to the natural world. Native Americans understood this. They held at their core the belief that all species are related. They also understood that a certain level of awareness must take place before we can truly communicate with that which is all around us.

It is not surprising, therefore, that in the folklore of every Native tribe are stories, tales, and beliefs to exemplify human's relationship to other animals. Native Americans lived with animals and within their environments. Animals were companions, adversaries, guides, advisors, and role models.

To most tribes, animals were great teachers, and the tribes' elders were their pupils. By careful observation and following their example, medicine people learned from the animals which plants were edible and which were poisonous. The animals provided insights about the seasons and migrations and wisdom about natural things.

Native Americans believed that animals regularly communicate with each other and sometimes with human beings. Many of the great medicine people of the past claimed to have spoken with one species of animal or another. Decisions affecting the whole tribe, such as those surrounding migrations, were often based on a message sent by a particular animal to an elder or spiritual leader. In fact, indigenous peoples around the globe have for centuries made decisions and based their lives on messages received from nature and the animal kingdom.

It is only now, in our technologically advanced culture—a culture in which we tend to believe only what we can see, prove, and explain—that we view animal-human communication as impossible or ludicrous. Yet the Dr. Dolittle philosophy is not so far-fetched. Many riders experience the apparent phenomenon of their horses doing exactly what the riders are thinking, seemingly at the same time they are thinking it, with no physical or verbal commands. These countless horse owners are not gurus, powerful medicine people, or psychics. They simply understand the relationship they have with their horses. The relationship between humans and other animals can be seen in many Native American stories and legends, which usually place emphasis on what can be learned from animals.

Few traditional legends contain references to the horse because Native contact with the horse was limited to only a few hundred years. When horses were first encountered, some tribes, thinking horses immortal, feared them. Many tribes viewed horses as big dogs. A few did not realize at first that horse and rider were two separate beings. Some tribes ate horses while others immediately saw in the horse a more efficient way of hunting. In light of all this, the Native Americans' ability and accomplishment with horses is even more remarkable.

How did horses come to live with Native Americans? Let's look at how horses first came to North America.

Native American Meets Horse

Horses existed in the Americas nearly forty million years ago, long before humans made their appearance. Over the millennia, *Equus caballus*, the ancient ancestor of the modern horse, migrated to Asia across the Bering land bridge that connected North America to Siberia. There *Equus caballus* continued to develop within its changing environment. Periodically, glacial melting submerged the Bering land bridge and all migration of mammals across its frozen terrain ceased. Sometime between 600,000 and 1,500,000 years ago, while the waters of the Bering Sea solidified into giant sheets of inland ice, the modern horse migrated back again from Asia to North America.

Then at the end of the Pleistocene epoch, about 10,000 years ago, the horse, along with many other species of mammals, mysteriously disappeared. The exact cause of this mass extinction is not known. What is known is from that time until about the middle of the sixteenth century there were no horses in North America.

In the late sixteenth and seventeenth centuries, waves of Spanish conquistadors arrived on the North American continent bringing horses with them. Christopher Columbus, Ponce de Leon, Vasquez de Ayllon, Panifilo de Narvarez, Alvar Nunez Cabeza de Vaca, Antonio de Mendoza, Hernandez De Soto all had horses on their explorations. In 1540, Francisco Vasquez de Coronado, twenty-nine-year-old governor of the most northern province of Mexico, led a contingent of 250 cavalrymen, 2,500 Nahuatl Atzecs and Africans, 500 pack animals, and 1,000 horses—mostly geldings, not stallions—northward into the American southwest, land of the Zunis.

The Spanish were bureaucrats. They kept scrupulous records and documented all exchanges of commodity with exacting standards. The horse was an important member of their culture. If anything happened to a horse on an expedition or in battle, it was noted in the records. And yet there is no record of any of Coronado's horses having escaped on his futile expedition.

Nor is there evidence that any of their horses were bred. In fact, many of the Spanish horses ended up as horse meat or horsehide boats for conquistadors.

Around 1600, mares and breeding stock started showing up in the northern Rio Grande colony, probably having been traded with the Spanish of northern Mexico. Foals were raised near Santa Fe and traded into the Plains nations. After the Native American success in the 1680 Pueblo revolt, horses were readily available to the Natives of the southwest. Horses were traded and some feral horses migrated northward until they reached the Blackfeet in Canada around the year 1710.

The breed first brought to the Americas by the Spaniards was the Spanish Barb. Called the horse of conquest, this small (14-14.2 hands), short, stocky, and rugged animal was originally brought to Spain from the Barbary Coast of Africa and subsequently to the New World. It was well known for its sure-footedness, endurance, and ability to forage for food on its own. The original Barb was probably closely related to the Berber horse,

an ancient breed with only five lumbar vertebrae. The horses first encountered by Native Americans of the Southwest and Plains were invariably Barbs or Barb crosses.

In the late seventeenth to eighteenth centuries, the French and English brought their breeds to North America. Among these were the "heavy" breeds such as the Suffolk Punch, Avelignese, Boulonnais, and Percheron. These horses interbred with the Barb, creating what is collectively termed the mustang. The mustang is a breed, but whether or not any true mustang stock still exists in North America is questionable.

The mustang has come to be associated with wildness. The word "mustang" is derived from the Spanish *musteños*, meaning stray. Most of the wild horses in North America are not wild at all, but feral—escaped domestic horses living in the wild. Many of these feral animals or their sires have been wild for only twenty years or less.

The reintroduction of the horse to North America, beginning in the mid-sixteenth century but becoming increasingly pronounced in the seventeenth century, had a significant impact on the western portion of this continent. Not only did horses directly affect the ecosystem by grazing, but they also brought with them European seed stock, parasites, fungi, and disease. By 1700, the grasses of the Great Plains had been overcome by immigrant species of plants.

Horses introduced in the east coast were used primarily as work animals, and although they greatly improved agricultural efforts, they did not have nearly the impact on the peoples and environment as horses did in the West.

The Impact of Horses on Native Life

For at least fourteen thousand years before the arrival of the horse, Native Americans used dogs in everyday life. Dogs were appreciated for their fidelity, enlisted to help with hunting, and transported family belongings. Occasionally during a special feast, they were eaten. Although Native Americans were never by definition nomadic, some tribes moved seasonally from place to place, summer camp to winter camp. When moving, two large sticks were crossed and tied to a dog's back, forming a travois on which family belongings could be lashed.

Using dogs as a beast of burden had its shortcomings, however. A dog could pack thirty to forty pounds at best, and travel only five to six miles per day. A dog needed to eat meat. Dogs often fought with each other, and if a rabbit should run across the path, a dog—along with all of its cargo—would take off after it.

Dogs were used extensively by Native Americans for hunting, but their abilities were limited. Dogs were no match for buffalo and could be used for hunting small game only. Native hunters allowed dogs to hunt in their natural pack formation, while standing by as a kill was made. This method of hunting was neither easy nor efficient.

When horses came along, it was only natural for many Native Americans to view them as big dogs. Throughout the Nations, the horse was called big dog, medicine dog, elk dog, spirit dog, and mysterious dog.

Natives immediately saw in the horse an opportunity to make life easier. A horse could pack two hundred pounds of belongings on his back or drag three hundred pounds on a travois. A horse could travel over twenty miles in a day and needed only grass to eat. And horses were relatively peaceful among themselves. Once tamed, horses were more dependable, easier to handle, bigger, and required less care than dogs.

With the horse came many new possibilities. On horseback, Natives could approach woodland animals as four-leggeds rather than two-leggeds. Buffalo could be chased and hunted with great speed, increasing a hunter's chance of success. Hunting territories expanded with the increased ability to track, chase, and successfully hunt bison.

Native Americans were inventive. For hunting, riderless horses were used as "runners." Runners were trained to run a herd of buffalo in the direction of the hunters while the hunters waited atop fresh mounts.

Horses were also used as a popular form of exchange among Native peoples. Horses were regularly traded and stolen, and they quickly became status symbols among the nations that utilized them. Chiefs sought to accumulate as many horses as possible. One band of two thousand Comanches had fifteen thousand horses! Some war chiefs personally possessed more than a thousand horses. Other chiefs wanted the best and fastest horses, not necessarily the most.

Many tribes created intricate breeding programs and practiced gelding to prevent horses with unwanted characteristics from perpetuating them. Beyond breeding for profit, Natives could now travel farther to trade and could migrate more easily, leaving behind their fiercest adversary, the weather.

At least two tribes bred horses for specific characteristics, thereby increasing their value on the open market. The Nez Percé (French for pierced nose)—originally members of the Palouse who broke away and relocated to the east—received as much as five times more for a Palouse horse than for any other. Their spotted horses came to be called Palousa, and finally they were named as we know them today, Appaloosa.

The other accomplished breeders were the Cayuse, who lived south and west of the Nez Percé. It is believed that the horses "found" by the Cayuse people were less desirable stock turned away by Nez Percé breeders. Cayuse horses, famous for their speed and endurance, were later sought after by the Pony Express. While the Cayuse horses were not pretty—usually gray, white, and brown—they were extremely fast. The word "Cayuse" was later used throughout the west to describe a wild, unbreakable horse.

Characteristics found desirable in horses varied from tribe to tribe and rider to rider. Some would not ride white horses. Others did not ride black horses. Some did not hunt with mares. Some preferred black hooves, others preferred white hooves. Some viewed blue-eyed horses as taboo, others viewed them as messengers. Ultimately, however, it was the temperament of the animal and not a specific physical characteristic that mattered most to the rider.

Spectacular relationships between horses and their riders are achieved today, but none of them exceed the relationship that was to be found between the Native American warrior and his pony.

The War Pony

Although most tribes did not corral or contain their horses, there was one exception: the war pony (called a pony by the French and English because of its size in comparison to the great draft animals of Europe). Most Native warriors kept their ponies tied or hobbled close to the lodge at all times. Some warriors would even bring their ponies into the lodge during bad weather, forcing the women and children to sleep elsewhere.

The war pony was chosen for its speed, agility, sure-footedness, tenacity, sensibility, endurance, and dependability, but above all, the pony was chosen for its temperament. The war pony had to have nerves of steel and yet the sense to "catch" its rider when he lost his balance. It needed unbridled speed and the ability to stand silently until led to do otherwise. More than anything, the war pony needed to be reliable. Mistakes in war translate to lost lives. War was simply no place for an unreliable mount.

This type of horse sounds ideal and maybe even unattainable, but understand that reliability describes any horse whose rider is concerned with having an understanding and oneness in action with his horse. Once they began to use and depend on horses, Native riders realized that their success and even their survival depended on the relationship they built with their horses.

War ponies were trained by their riders, sometimes over many years. Looking back, we may think that in those days riders had more time to work with their horses. Not true. Sixteen to eighteen hours of survival work on a daily basis is not exactly free time. Those of us who work forty hours a week probably have twice as much time for our horses than did the average Native

American horseman. Those horsemen understood that without a healthy working relationship with their horses, they had better not go to war.

A warrior's ability to communicate with his horse was one of the most valuable skills he could develop. Other tribal members often thought horsemen to be imperious or reclusive because they placed so much importance on this relationship. It has been said that the most frequent argument between a horseman and his wife was over the war pony.

If you can develop with your horse just a little bit of the type of relationship that Native riders had with their ponies, you may also become addicted to this rapport. The war pony was companion, best friend, soul mate, and teacher. Most important, the war pony was kola: a friend with whom you could face many encircling enemies. The word "kola" is not normally used for animals but is reserved for human brother-warriors. In using kola as a descriptor of their relationship to their horses, Native American warriors acknowledged their horses' equal status as brother-warrior.

Horse Painting and Decorating

Native Americans painted their horses with special symbolic medicine paints to intimidate the enemy, give their horses strength and courage in battle, and advertise the achievements of both rider and horse.

The medicine paint was made up of varying natural pigments. Ash for white or gray; charcoal for black; berries for reds, blues, and purples; ocher for yellow. These natural pigments were blended with either water or animal fat to make paint. The Plains warriors often painted the same symbols on themselves as they did on the flanks and necks of their horses. Among others, there were marks for medicine men, mourning, and horse raids.

War paint was a badge or medal that indicated particular acts of prowess. Each symbol had its own meaning that was known to all members of the horse culture. A circle placed around the eye of the horse served to give the horse better vision. Upside down horseshoes indicated how many horse raids the rider had participated in. A design shaped like a keyhole placed on the horse by a medicine person or spiritual leader was a blessing and protector. Handprints indicated the number of enemies killed by the rider in hand-to-hand combat without the aid of weapons. Stacked horizontal lines counted coup.

Coup, a French word meaning touch, was a way of dishonoring the enemy by touching him. The belief that a warrior could obtain some of the

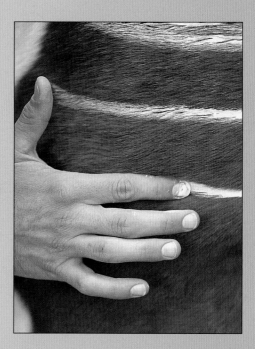

soul of his enemy, as well as some of his strength, courage, and energy, motivated warriors to count coup whenever the opportunity arose. Coup did not always precede the death of the enemy but was also used as a warning to the enemy to get out of Native American territory.

Native Americans also wove things into their war ponies' manes or tails. A lock of the rider's own hair was tied into the mane of his pony so their spirits could be one. A feather from a hawk, eagle, or falcon (all considered to be war birds) gave the horse the speed and agility of that bird. Hail marks, made famous by Crazy Horse, were believed to give the horse and rider the strength and fury of a great hail storm.

Relationship Training

After training many horses and many riders, I noticed a pattern developing. Although the riders enjoyed working with and riding their horses, there were always problems. Probably the most common phone call that I received was the request to "come and fix my horse."

Whether it was a horse who spooked easily or one who would not get into a trailer, it seemed that every single horse owner had at least one problem with a horse who needed to be fixed.

My first position was to attack the communication problem that inherently exists between horse and human. Perhaps the riders were not communicating in such a way that the horses could understand.

I sought advice. I thought. I began to look at what it was that I did differently to achieve results with horses. Finally, it dawned on me. Those horse owners were having so many problems because "a horse is a horse!" That's it. If we can understand what it means to be a horse, react like a horse, and relate to other things like a horse, then we can have a more productive relationship with a horse.

Native Americans knew that a horse is a horse, which helps explain why Native American riders were so successful with horses in such a short amount of time. Native Americans were extremely practical and intuitively understood the deeper significance of things. Looking at the horse, Native Americans evaluated and defined its nature and moved forward using that definition. They did not attempt to treat the horse as they would a dog or a human, but instead trained, rode, and communicated within the boundaries set forth by the nature of the horse.

I began to understand that almost every problem faced by the horse owner (excluding physical injuries or ailments) was due to an unbalanced relationship between horse and rider. In most cases, riders were not fulfilling the position in the relationship that horses needed them to. A horse needs a leader. If he does not have a leader, he will become the leader. In fact, the success a rider has in his relationship with his horse is proportionate to the degree in which the rider is able to be the leader.

I believe the relationship between horse and rider, more than anything else, is what determines the ability to achieve results. In the horse's world, the relationship with all other members of the herd is the foundation supporting every move and decision a horse makes throughout his life. The relationship between horse and rider is the beginning. The beginning is a good place to start.

Relationship Training is more than a collection of methods or techniques for training your horse. It is an attitude or belief system that can be applied to all methods and techniques of horsemanship. It embodies two basic understandings. One is knowing that the boundaries and behaviors inherent in the horse's life as a herd animal facilitates our communication and actions with our horse. The other basic understanding is knowing that it is more important and more productive to concentrate on the relationship between human and animal than it is to concentrate on the results that we hope to achieve.

At the very foundation of Relationship Training is the connectedness of all life and the respect with which we, as humans, must treat the animals of our larger family. The winged animals of the air, the four-leggeds, and the fish in the waters are our brothers and sisters. Once we realize and act as though we understand this relationship, and once we accept the responsibility to all our animal brothers and sisters that goes along with this relationship, then true training can begin. Because in truth, training is nothing other than attunement. Attunement of rider to horse and attunement of horse to rider.

The buffalo will disappear, at last, and another animal will take its place,

a slick animal with a long tail and split hoofs, whose flesh you will learn to eat.

But first there will be another animal you must learn to use.

It has a shaggy neck and a tail almost touching the ground. Its hoofs are round.

This animal will carry you on his back and help you in many ways.

Those far hills that seem only a blue vision in the distance take many days to reach now,

but with this animal you can get there in a short time, so fear him not.

—SWEET MEDICINE, *CULTURAL HERO OF THE CHEYENNE*

1

Hunkapi (hoon-KAH-pee)
I Am Related to Everyone

I t is virtually impossible to understand horses from a Native American perspective without first understanding how Natives view their relationship to all animals.

Sometime after the mid-sixteenth century, a growing number of people in North America were introduced to two notions. These two notions were that humans and nature are not related, and that humans hold the highest position on earth according to Creator's ladder. We Native Americans know this idea was brought to the New World by the Europeans.

Prior to this way of thinking, Native Americans viewed themselves as an integral part of nature, having an equal share—along with everything else in the universe—of the earth. Although Native Americans believed that they were charged with the stewardship of the earth and its animals, they did not believe that they were to rule, subdue, or preside over it.

Animals on the most fundamental level are either hunter or hunted. This fact, more than any other single characteristic, determines the relationship between species, human beings included. If we are to develop a healthy working relationship with an animal, we must first understand how that animal views us. If the animal in question views us as a hunter, its natural fear and apprehension must be overcome for it to exhibit trust toward us. If the animal views us as hunted, there is a certain amount of respect we must earn before a relationship can be established.

Horses are hunted—humans are hunters. Humans look like hunters, act like hunters, move like hunters, sound like hunters, and even smell like hunters. Now imagine you are a rabbit. Along comes a wolf who wants to gain your trust. You know very well that wolves eat rabbits, and initially you avoid the wolf. Yet this wolf seems sincere in his efforts to build a relationship with you. The apprehension you would feel in that situation is the same apprehension your horse feels until he trusts you.

From your horse's point of view, you could have him for dinner at any given moment. If you have ever become angry or frustrated with your horse and perhaps yelled or snapped, you may have witnessed your horse shifting his weight to his hindquarters, lifting his chin, looking down at you

Gluscabi and the Game Animals

Abenaki, Northeast Woodland

Long ago, Gluscabi decided he would do some hunting. He took his bow and arrows and went into the woods. But all the animals saw him coming and hid from him.

Gluscabi could not find them. He was not pleased. He went home to the little lodge near the big water where he lived with Grandmother Woodchuck.

"Grandmother," he said, "make a game bag for me." So Grandmother Woodchuck took caribou hair and made him a game bag. She wove it together tight and strong, and it was a fine game bag. But when she gave it to Gluscabi, he threw it down.

"This is not good enough, Grandmother," he said. So she used moose hair and wove him another game bag, large and strong. She flattened porcupine quills with her teeth and she wove a design into the game bag to make it even more attractive.

But Gluscabi threw it down. "Grandmother," he said, "this is not good enough."

"Eh, Gluscabi," said Grandmother Woodchuck, "how can I please you? What kind of game bag do you want?" Gluscabi smiled. "Ah, Grandmother," he said, "make one out of woodchuck hair."

So Grandmother Woodchuck pulled all of the hair from her belly. (To this day, woodchucks have no hair there.) She wove it into a magic game bag. No matter how much was put into it, there was still room for more.

Gluscabi smiled. "*Oleohneh*, Grandmother," he said. "I thank you." He went back into the woods and came to a large clearing. He called out as loudly as he could, "All you animals, listen to me. A terrible thing is going to happen. The sun is going to go out. The world is going to end, and everything is going to be destroyed."

The animals became frightened. They came to the clearing. "Gluscabi," they said, "what can we do? The world is going to be destroyed. How can we survive?"

Gluscabi smiled. "My friends," he said, "just climb into my game bag. You will be safe in there when the world is destroyed."

So all the animals went into his game bag. The rabbits and the squirrels went in, and the game bag stretched to hold them. The raccoons and the foxes went in, and the game bag stretched larger still. The deer and the caribou went in. The bears went in and the moose went in, and the game bag stretched to hold them all. Soon, all the animals in the world were in the bag. Gluscabi tied the top of the game bag, laughed, and slung it over his shoulder and went home.

"Grandmother," he said, "now we no longer have to look for food. Whenever we want anything to eat, we can just reach into my game bag."

Grandmother Woodchuck opened Gluscabi's game bag and looked inside. There were all the game animals in the world. "Oh, Gluscabi," she said, "you cannot keep all these animals in a bag. They will sicken and die. There will be none left for our children and our children's children. It is right that it should be difficult to hunt them. It makes you stronger by trying to find them, and the animals grow stronger and wiser trying to avoid being caught. This is the right balance."

"*Kaamoji*, Grandmother," said Gluscabi, "that is so." So he picked up his game bag and went back to the clearing. He opened it up. "All you animals," he called out, "you can come out now. Everything is all right. The world was destroyed, but I put it back together again."

All the animals came out of the magic game bag. They went back into the woods, and they are still there today because Gluscabi heard what his Grandmother Woodchuck had to say.

with fearful eyes, and trying to turn or back out of the situation. In that moment, your horse has exhibited his nature as a hunted animal.

One would think that it would be easier to establish a relationship with a hunted animal. Trust is easily gained in prey animals simply by letting the animals know we are not going to harm them. There is another hurdle we must overcome with the hunted animal.

Many hunted animals are also herd animals and spend most of their lives defending their position within the herd. Behavior of a herd animal, especially an animal who is in a position to reprimand, can easily be confused by humans as predator behavior. Vicious attacks, including biting, kicking, chasing, and stomping, occur often. In the herd, an ongoing pecking order is enforced and reinforced. It is the herd members' responsibility to constantly challenge the leadership abilities of other herd members with higher rank. This constant insubordination insures that the most qualified are given the higher positions in the herd.

Along comes the human.

In an attempt to develop a relationship with a hunted herd animal such as the horse, the human must not only give the animal a reason to feel secure, but must maintain the status of leader, alpha, or itancan, in the herd—a herd of two, rider and horse. This can become tricky, and the scales are not balanced in the human's favor.

If you have ever felt while training or riding that your horse is getting the better of you, acting spoiled, or just not paying attention, you are probably losing your status as itancan of your two-member herd. This behavior is usually nothing more than your horse getting comfortable with, and enjoying, his new status.

In the very beginning of relationship development, it is important for you to be the leader your horse is looking for. When you and your horse are standing in a training arena, your horse will usually first exhibit his leadership qualities by walking or trotting, high headed, around you. When you do not follow as he expects you to, he may begin to question his own position in the herd. He will begin to pay more attention to you by pivoting an ear toward you, looking at you, or possibly turning to face you. At this moment, take the leadership position by physically putting yourself in a position of leadership. Walk in front of your horse expecting him to follow, and he will.

Awi Usdi, Little Deer

Cherokee, North Carolina

Back when the world was young, the humans and the animal people could speak to each other. At first they lived in peace. The humans hunted the animals only when they needed food or skins to make clothing. Then the humans discovered the bow and arrow. With this new weapon, they could kill many animals quickly and with great ease. They began to kill animals when they did not need them for food or clothing. It seemed as if all the animals in the world would soon be exterminated.

The animals met in council. The bears decided they would have to fight back. "How can we do that?" said one of the bear warriors. "The humans will shoot us with their arrows before we come close to them." Old Bear, their chief, agreed. "That is true," he said. "We must learn how to use the same weapons they use." The bears made a very strong bow and fashioned arrows for it. But whenever they tried to use the bow, their long claws got in the way. "I will cut off my claws," said one of the bear warriors. He did so, and he was able to use the bow and arrow. His aim was good and he hit his mark every time.

"That is good," said Old Bear. "Now can you climb this tree?" The bear tried to climb the tree, but he failed. Old Bear shook his head. "This will not do. Without our claws, we cannot climb trees or hunt or dig for food. We must give up this idea of using the same weapons the humans use."

One by one, each of the animal groups met. One by one, they came to no conclusion. It seemed there was no way to fight back. But the last group to meet were the deer. Awi Usdi, Little Deer, was their leader. "I see what we must do," he said. "We cannot stop the humans from hunting animals. That is the way it was meant to be. However, the humans are not doing things in the right way. If they do not respect us and hunt us when there is no real need, they may kill us all. I shall go now and tell the hunters what they must do. Whenever they wish to kill a deer, they must prepare a ceremony. They must ask me for permission to kill one of us. After they kill a deer,

they must show respect to its spirit and ask for pardon. If they do not do this, I shall track them down, and with my magic I will make their limbs crippled. Then they will no longer be able to walk or shoot a bow and arrow."

Awi Usdi, Little Deer, did as he said. At night, he whispered into the ears of the hunters, telling them what they must do. When they awoke, some of the hunters thought they had been dreaming and they were not sure that the dream was a true one. Others, though, realized that Awi Usdi, Little Deer, had spoken to them. They did as he told them. They hunted for the deer and other animals only when they needed food and clothing. They remembered to prepare in a ceremonial way, to ask permission before killing an animal, and to ask pardon when an animal was killed.

The others continued to kill animals for no reason. Awi Usdi, Little Deer, came to them and, using his magic, crippled them with rheumatism. Before long, all of the hunters began to treat the animals with respect and followed Awi Usdi, Little Deer's, teachings.

So it is that the animals have survived to this day. Because of Awi Usdi, Little Deer, the Indian people show respect. To this day, even though the animals and people no longer can speak to each other as in the old days, the people still show respect and give thanks to the animals they must hunt.

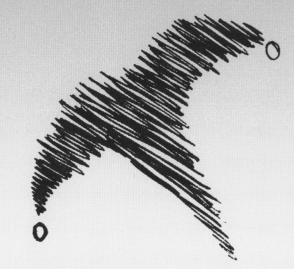

Woksapa [wo-K'SAH-pah]
WISDOM

Through oral tradition, wisdom among Native Americans was a cumulative process. Wisdom of the elders was passed down to the next generation so that it could be added to the experiences of those people. Native American wisdom about animals and our relationship to them was above and beyond that of many cultures. From this wisdom we can learn many things.

Beyond hunter-hunted relationships are complex understandings that are made clear by the Native American view of animals. All animals, living on, in, or above Mother Earth, have always been viewed by Native Americans as brothers and sisters. The words "brothers and sisters" are used here in a very literal sense and should not be confused as esoteric niceties. Animals were viewed, treated, and respected by Native Americans in the same way as they treated their genetic brothers and sisters.

The brothers and sisters of the animal kingdom were viewed by most tribal members in one of three ways—as guides, companions, or creatures needing protection. Just as you would respect and seek guidance from an older sibling or relative, so did most Native tribes seek wisdom from animals viewed as guides. The friendship found in a relative of like age is the same friendship found in animals viewed as companions. The responsibility felt toward a younger sibling is the same as the sense of responsibility for providing shelter to those species called the ones to be protected.

If you have ever experienced a long-term relationship with a dog, cat, horse, or other animal, you probably know the brotherly love and rapport that accompanies this relationship. Native Americans see all living things with the same intensity as you see your special pet. Every bird, fish, rock, or plant is given the same respect and admiration as you would give a very close family member. This philosophy was commonplace and taken for granted—an understanding that supported the core beliefs of the indigenous peoples in North America.

Although horses were viewed by Native Americans as companions and animals to be cared for, more often than not the horse was more of a messenger, teacher, or guide than it was a student. Too often, modern-day riders view their animals as students and can't seem to understand why those animals don't "get it," when in fact, their horses already know it. Believe it or not, many horse owners have said, "my horse does not know how to go right," or "my horse won't stop." Think about these statements for a moment. Horses know how to do everything that is possible for them to do from the day that they are born. It is the rider who has the deficiency in communicating requests. Horses do not need to be taught how to stop, turn, or spin around in a circle. Riders must be taught how to communicate these requests to their horses in an understandable way.

Native American riders, who only had access to horses for one hundred fifty to two hundred years, did one thing better than most, thereby becoming the greatest horsemen this continent has ever seen—they viewed their horses as guides and they listened to their horses.

Among many of the tribes and Nations there is a common custom that trains an individual from a young age to listen. This custom takes on different forms in different tribes, but it is exemplified by what's called the talking stick, a short stick of twelve to eighteen inches, usually decorated with carvings. The person holding the stick is the only person permitted to talk. Once that person has finished, the stick is passed to the next person to talk. In the unlikely event that someone should interrupt the person holding the stick, the speaker would point at the violator. The embarrassment associated with this infraction was usually enough to make the offender get up and leave the room.

It is said that the reason Creator gave two-leggeds two ears and one mouth was so that we could listen twice as much as we talk. Start listening.

Listen! Or your Tongue

will make you deaf.

—Cherokee Saying

Nioeye Weksuye [nee-OH-yay week-soo-yay]
YOUR WORDS I WILL REMEMBER

There is only one thing that stands between a horse and a rider performing as one creature. Only one hurdle separates the perfect combination of two- and four-legged. One stumbling block awaiting the horse and rider who wish to act as one. It is communication. A horse and rider who can communicate successfully can do anything. Anything!

Many people are awed at the things that great trainers can do with their horses. One Mexican charro can make his horse lie down and stay down for over five minutes without ever touching the horse. Some horses can make hairpin turns at breakneck speed around barrels. Reining horses slide over twenty feet on packed soil to a stop. Some horses can jump over fences that are over seven feet tall.

Great trainers are great communicators. Horses know how to jump. They know how to stop, run, turn, sidepass, piaffe, go backward, and lie down. If a horse knows how to stop, and if you want the horse to stop, all you have to do is effectively communicate this. The horse will stop (considering that pain or fear is not involved) only if a healthy working relationship has been established between horse and rider.

Modern riders use a variety of training methods that aren't always the best way of communicating with a horse. Two popular methods are "telling" and "asking."

Telling is the most widespread way riders communicate to their horses. Most of us have been conditioned to understand that telling is what animals understand best. We say sit, stay, giddyap, whoa, roll over, come, heel, back up. This is the way most people train their animals; they tell them what to do and expect them to obey. When you do what you are told, you are rewarded. When you disobey, you are punished. Within this situation, there is no room for opinion, judgment, intuition, expression, or instinct. You are merely performing a task because someone is telling you to do it. How do you feel when you are around someone who is always telling you what to do?

The problem with telling as communication is that the only two options given for performance are reward and punishment. The reward is

not necessarily something you want, but rather something the teller wishes to give you. The negative support of punishment is nothing more than do this or you will suffer in some way. Have you ever raised your hand in anger as if you were about to hit your horse? You may find that in the future just the raising of your hand will cause a shying away.

Horses have incredible memories. If intelligence were purely graded on the ability to recall and utilize information, I believe horses would be considered far more intelligent than humans. It is very important to be aware of the memory power of the horse when training, especially when communicating your requests.

More often than not, the reward for obedience is nothing more than not being punished. For example, you kick your horse to get him moving. If your horse begins to walk, the reward is that life goes on without reprimand. If your horse does not begin to walk, he gets kicked harder. In effect, the only reason your horse moves at all is to avoid being kicked more severely.

Telling does not make for a very good relationship with your horse. As a matter of fact, it makes for no type of relationship whatsoever.

Asking has its place in communication, but asking can be a trap. Although asking is a nice way to try to get your horse to do something, most riders, unfortunately, ask in the wrong way and for the wrong reasons. The asking technique is used primarily in two situations both of which are usually ineffective.

In one situation, you are very attached to your horse or view your horse as a pet much like a house cat. You believe that because you and the horse are such good friends, a mere verbal request will result in the horse doing what you ask. Because the horse does not understand the human language, and because you may not know what the horse does comprehend, your efforts are futile at best. Although this asking technique is well intentioned, horses need more than just a cosmic connection with their riders to understand what is being asked.

You must so that your words may go as sunlight

The other situation is the when-all-else-fails exercise. It goes something like this. You nudge your horse's sides with your heel and your horse doesn't respond. You then give the horse a good stiff kick in the ribs (the telling method of communication). Still, your horse stands and up goes the head. You then decide that in order to get this animal moving, you must convey the message more intensely. By lifting your boot, you are able to land a good solid jab to the horse's side. You probably end up on the ground as the dust settles. You climb back onto the horse's back realizing that a new technique must be utilized. After a few deep breaths, you begin the when-all-else-fails asking technique. Giddyap girl? Come on!? You can do it!? Giddyap!? Walk? Pleeeeeeease?? Your horse has a good chuckle at your expense.

The "wishing" and "hoping" techniques are offshoots of the asking technique. Asking your horse nicely, even with the best intentions, cannot be relied on to produce results. A relationship must exist and you must know how to communicate effectively with your horse.

speak straight

to our hearts.

—Cochise, Chiricahua Apache

Itancan [ee-TAHN-chun] and *Waunca* [wah-OON-chah]
Leader and Imitator

Native American riders knew the nature of the medicine dog. Most of the horse's nature stems from the horse being a herd animal. In a herd, the *itancan* leads and all other members of the herd follow. The herd knows their itancan has their best interests in mind. You are the itancan of your two-member herd. It is only natural that your horse will follow your lead for he knows you have his best interests in mind.

It is important you understand the psychology behind waunca. It is the responsibility of waunca to follow itancan without regard to the outcome of itancan's actions. If waunca did not blindly follow itancan, the purpose of the herd would be defeated and eventually the species would die out.

There is a lot more than most people realize to the saying "you can lead a horse to water but you can't make him drink." It is possible, though, to lead a horse to drink. When a herd of horses approaches a watering hole, the itancan always approaches the water in front of the herd. The itancan checks for danger and then takes a few sips. Only then will the rest of the herd take its fill, as the itancan backs off and watches for predators. After the herd has finished drinking and the itancan feels all is safe, then—and only then—will he go back to the water and drink until his thirst is quenched. The itancan has led horses to water and led them to drink.

By being the itancan of your herd, you can achieve the same result in any number of training exercises. Once you are established as the itancan, your horse will always look to you for guidance and direction.

Iyuptala [ee-yoo-P'TAH-lah]
ONE WITH

Being "one with" was integral to Native American life. Life was lived in the understanding that the people were one with their environment. They were one with Mother Earth. They were one with the elements, and, above all, one with Creator. So basic was this way of being in the world that certain words such as trust, integrity, belief, faith, and promise simply did not exist. The concepts behind them were meaningless. As every action reflected the Native American's total trust in the environment, a breech in that trust was regarded as unthinkable. Trust and integrity were not the exception but the rule.

Native Americans exhibited the same type of trust that was shown to them by natural things. Never will you touch a fire that will not burn you. Never will you see rain that is not wet, and never will you see a wolf who is really a sheep. Natural things do not lie.

The type of trust that is exhibited by natural things is entirely different from human trust. We must understand both types of trust before we embark on a relationship with our horses.

Unfortunately, the experience of being "one with" has been lost by the majority of people living in the twentieth century. Far from feeling at one with our environment, one with Mother Earth, or even one with Creator, we learn from a very young age to trust nothing that has not first earned our trust. Most animals, on the other hand, are born with the understanding to trust everything until there is a reason not to trust. Native Americans learned to trust in the "animal" way. Once they were given very good reasons not to trust, it was too late.

In May of 1966, an expedition to the Galápagos Islands revealed evidence that animals trust humans until they are given a reason not to. Scientists were amazed at how the animals of the islands showed no intimidation to their presence. Birds landed on their shoulders, and the scientists could sunbathe alongside the sea lions. Any species, even those with young, could be approached without difficulty. It was not until the scientists began collecting, tagging, and trapping the animals that their behavior changed dramatically. After the animals were given a reason not to trust, they began treating humans as predators rather than cohabitants.

The scientists on that expedition discovered that the apprehension shown to them after they had breached trust was not hereditary. A newborn animal's tendency to flee from a human is not due to its ancestry or genes, but to observing its parents fleeing. Newborn animals found away from their parents could be approached, touched, and held. They exhibited trusting behavior toward the scientists.

Another example of this natural trust is evident in the relationships turtles have with most animals. Most turtles and tortoises have managed somehow to retain the trust of much of the animal kingdom. Because they have never breached this trust, they are generally treated with indifference. If for some reason turtles and tortoises across the globe started biting the toes and legs and fins of passers-by, the animal kingdom's attitude toward turtles and tortoises would change. Animals exhibiting predator behavior, in this case the turtles and tortoises, experience an immediate and violent response to their behavior.

The horse, when weighed on a trust scale (if there were such a thing), would fall somewhere between a dog and cow. Most horses are very trusting, yet it does not take much for them to lose that trust. This concept must be in the forefront of your mind whenever you are in the presence of your horse.

Your horse's trust in you can be lost in any number of ways. Lose your temper and hit your horse on the head, and you are well on your way to creating a head-shy horse who will not trust you to touch his head again. Trust can be lost when you load your horse into an unsafe trailer with a jagged piece of metal on which he cuts his leg. It can be lost when your horse strains a tendon after you've urged him down a hill he is not able to safely or confidently negotiate. In each of these examples, the trust between horse and rider was breached by the rider.

Remember, you are the itancan. You have chosen and earned that title with the stipulation that you will lead the herd safely. If you begin to breach that trust by not acting responsibly and in the itancan manner, you will be replaced. Who will replace you? The other member of your herd, your horse.

To understand what it means to be "one with," reflect for a moment on an eagle soaring with the currents. The eagle does not glide on top of or below or alongside those currents, but is actually enveloped within them. Every shift in the wind affects the eagle and every beat of the eagle's wings moves the currents around him. Every move that one makes affects the other. The eagle becomes a small part of the winds. His movements reflect the movements of the ever shifting winds of which he has become a part. The soaring eagle knows what it means to be one with the wind.

2

The Basis for Relationship Training

Relationship Training is concerned with the relationship between horse and human more than it is concerned with any immediate, hoped for results. Remember, a horse is a horse. Rather than work within a human behavioral framework, Relationship Training uses the relationship, language, and boundaries a horse understands best—the herd—as a setting in which its techniques and exercises occur.

In Relationship Training, we realize that no horse will ever learn that which we hope to teach in the amount of time we hope to teach it. If a strong working relationship is our long-term goal, we had better avoid frustrations during the training process. Relationship Training is not rider teaching horse. Nor is it horse teaching rider. Rather, it is creating the right environment. A right environment creates the most productive set of emotional and physical boundaries possible. It creates an environment in which two beings can understand each other.

JUST AS THE NATIVE AMERICAN RIDER'S ABILITY TO COMMUNI-
CATE WITH HORSES WAS NOTHING SHORT OF SPECTACULAR, SO
WAS THE HORSE'S ABILITY TO INTERPRET COMMANDS GIVEN ON AN
instant's notice. Because they were iyuptala, "one with," each other, horse
and rider teams navigated treacherous terrain daily; rode among a herd of a
thousand stampeding bison; and descended near-vertical slopes, sometimes
fleeing from an enemy. If at any time horse and rider were not thinking and
responding as one unit, injury or death to one or both of them was likely.

The ability to act as one with one's horse is the most sought-after
skill for riders of all disciplines at all levels. It requires open, two-way communication between horse and rider. It can easily be obtained, but by no
means does it come quickly. To secure a true partnering relationship and
forge open communication with your horse, very specific tools are needed,
the most important of which is time.

Certain
small ways
and observances
sometimes have
connection with large

Time

The specialized tool most critical in communicating with your horse openly is time. Time is also the single most important tool when developing a oneness with our horse. Let's take a look at just how much and what kind of time was spent by the continent's greatest horsemen with their horses.

Imagine you are a Native American living in the year 1760. Thus far, European contact has been minimal. You and your family live in a camp along with eighty or so other families on the shoal of a shallow western river. Your horses (not hobbled or tied) are perfectly content to share with you the meadows found just outside of camp. As you gather herbs and berries, the four-legged members of your tribe graze at your side and curious yearlings nudge you in hopes of a sweet-berry. While you bathe, the itancan leads the herd to the river, and when the horses have quenched their thirst, the itancan takes a drink as well. Occasionally, a foal bounds through camp with children close behind trying to grab her short, wiry tail.

Your nights are spent sleeping in your family lodge, a cone-shaped tepee. Through the smoke opening at the top of the tepee, you can see the stars. The constant murmur of the herd provides a background for your every thought and dream. A *sakehanska* (sha-KAY-hahn-SKAH—a long-claws, or grizzly bear) approaches the camp. With grunts and whinnies the herd alerts everyone to the danger. The young men silently leave the tepees to frighten the predator away. When they have returned, you can hear the mares calming and reassuring their young.

and more profound ideas.

—STANDING BEAR

It was not until I had the opportunity to spend two years traveling, and giving clinics and seminars, that I came to appreciate the impact that time had on my relationship with my horse. I lived in the front half of a sixteen-foot gooseneck stock trailer, and my horse Kola lived in the back. Our quarters were separated by a steel bar that came up to Kola's chest. I soon learned that, like humans, Kola snored and grunted in his sleep, had nightmares, and occasionally woke me up for that proverbial drink of water. Living with a horse, you learn to recognize moods, contentment,

(continued at right)

Think for a moment about what kind of relationship you would have with your horse if you both lived under these circumstances. Witnessing his emotions and response to the daily multitude of events, you would come to a greater knowingness about your horse—and to a deeper appreciation.

Time well spent with your horse means much more than performing daily tasks in his presence. It means time spent observing him; it means unencumbered time spent living near him, for there are many things about your horse that you don't and can't know unless you spend time together.

Surveys have shown that most horse owners spend an average of six hours per week in the presence of their horses. Two of these six hours are typically spent working in barns and stalls, and on fences; one hour is spent feeding and watering the horses; one hour is spent grooming; and the remaining two hours are spent on the horses' backs.

Let's put this in perspective from the horse's point of view. Imagine the kind of relationship you'd have with a spouse with whom you spent two hours every week doing the laundry, one hour at dinner, one hour on the couch watching television, and two hours driving around a major city to which you've both never been, trying to decipher directions and read a map.

Your horse looks and yearns for leadership, companionship, and a relationship with you. If you spend only a little time developing that relationship with your horse, it will not be a strong one. Spending minimal time together does not promote oneness. It's not hard to understand why most horse owners who lack oneness with their horses have communication problems.

The time we spend with our horses must be time devoted to nurturing our relationship with them. We want to strengthen the bonds of friendship and understanding and facilitate communication. And what makes for good time spent with your horse? Motivation. The motivation to spend time with your horse solely to develop a relationship with him. Our actions reflect our motives. If your desire to develop a relationship with your horse is nothing more than a good intention, then the time to do so will elude you.

Your time together is not just time when you happen to be in the same space. Hand grazing, taking a walk, grooming (for no purpose other than to connect with your horse), and hanging out in the pasture are all opportunities to deepen the relationship with your horse. Barn chores, feeding, and mindless longeing are not.

boredom, frustration—basically, the same things you'd learn about a human were you to spend a lot of time together. Initially, when Kola shifted his weight, I jumped out of a deep sleep, banging my head on the ceiling of my sleeping area. But I became accustomed to Kola's sleeping habits in about a month, and soon found no reason to trade in our two-bedroom condominium-on-wheels. I'm glad I didn't, because living in such close quarters with my horse enabled me to learn a valuable lesson: When developing a relationship with your horse, there is no substitute for spending time together.

Communication

Generally, your messages to your horse can be conveyed in three ways: verbally, physically, and focally. Focal messages are those that are communicated by merely focusing your attention or energy in a particular direction. Especially in the beginning stages of training, a combination of verbal, physical, and focal messages are usually necessary.

Visualize a scale of one to ten that indicates the urgency of a message you give your horse, with ten being the most urgent. A focal message is about a three on the scale, a physical message is a six, and a verbal message is a nine or ten. Without a scale of urgency, all messages are communicated as equal, and your horse will become bored or confused. For instance, if you use the same message—at the same intensity—to slow your horse to a walk as you do to avoid running into a briar patch, you will end up with many thorns in your britches. However, if you yell "whoa" every time you would like to slow down a little bit, your horse will begin tuning out your requests. You will be ignored, like the boy who cried wolf. Horses are dynamic creatures and must be communicated to as such. They are intelligent enough to respond to different degrees of the same stimulus.

Horses depend primarily on body language to convey messages; they are not primarily vocal creatures the way humans are. Verbal commands are most effective when used to communicate urgent information. The most appropriate instances in which to use verbal commands are when you want to stop or start abruptly. Many riders cluck to their horses to go from a standstill to a walk. When they want to go into a trot, they squeeze their legs, take more contact with the reins, lean forward, push with their seats, and cluck. The cluck is the same vocal cue used to get into the walk.

What these riders do not usually understand is that in many cases their horses have learned to do two things on their own. The first is to disregard the noises their riders make (because they're ever-present), and the second is to pay more attention to physical and focal messages. The riders

The concept of nonverbal communication is simple in practice but extremely difficult to explain. I did not fully understand this concept until I was put into a potentially dangerous situation with my horse. Two years before this incident, the concept had been explained to me by a Cheyenne woman.

This is what happened. One March morning in Florida, some friends of mine returned from a trail ride. I had not gone with them but went to greet them when they came into view. One woman at the rear was riding a green mustang from the Bureau of Land Management. With no apparent provocation, the mustang threw his head violently, breaking the mechanical hackamore. I believe the horse saw this failure of equipment as his opportunity to return to the Great Plains—he threw his rider and hightailed it down the road. I jumped on Kola and soon caught up with the galloping mustang. Kola loves a good chase, so he was really into chasing this mustang. I tried to stay back about twenty to thirty yards so that I could be there

(continued at right)

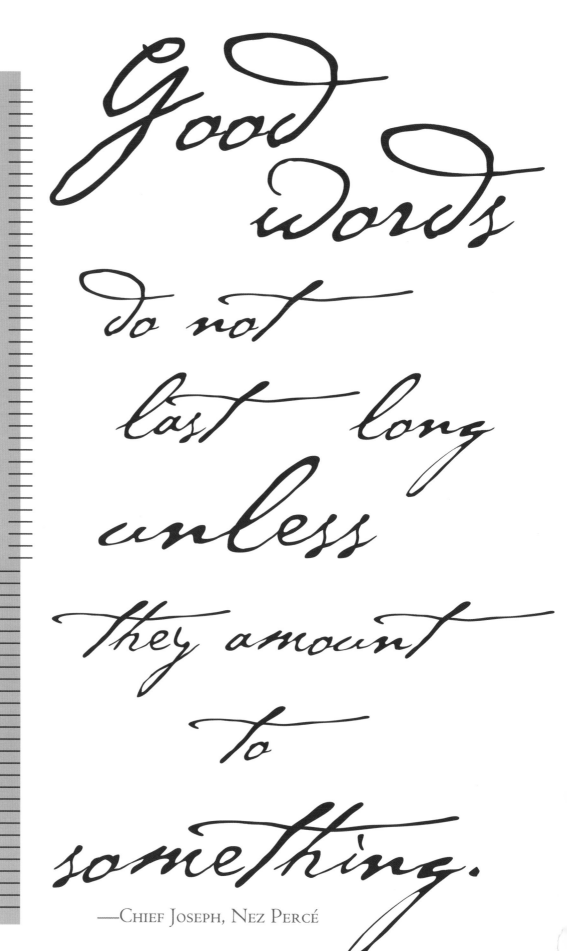

Good words do not last long unless they amount to something.

—CHIEF JOSEPH, NEZ PERCÉ

usually have no idea what is going on in their horses' heads. They use the approach that a few clucks are like changing gears on a manual transmission. They miss the point at which their horses start understanding and anticipating more subtle messages. Horses, like all prey animals, respond to foreign noises instinctively.

The human voice is a powerful conveyor of messages. Use it only when it is necessary. The other member of your herd usually only vocalizes to establish territory, convey danger, or comfort peers. Your horse might think you are schizophrenic if you talk too much!

Physical messages, a five or six on the communication scale are the most effective form of communication in most situations. This is especially true when riding bareback. When sitting on our horses' backs, we are constantly sending messages to them. Learning to recognize and effectively communicate these messages are the core teachings of Relationship Training. Some of the messages that physical communication conveys are stand, stop, start, slow down, speed up, step, jump, turn, and back up.

Being the hunted, horses are acutely aware of their surroundings at all times. They are also amply aware of everything their riders are doing. A slight shift of your weight, depending on the direction and degree, can cue your horse to do any number of things such as turn, switch leads, or collect in a turn.

A horse also can recognize anxieties and desires through physical messages. Usually, without being aware of it, we convey physical messages to our horses. Being able to recognize these physical cues and use them as communication tools does away with the need to consciously communicate our requests. When you become aware of these cues and use them to communicate, you and your horse will act as one.

Focus is a three on the communication scale only because of the intensity needed to convey messages with focus. You've experienced focus before; it is what you feel or sense when someone out of your field of vision is watching you. Focus is an ability that both humans and horses possess. It is most evident in intense or dangerous situations.

when the mustang became trapped or tired enough to stop. He ran full speed into a garage. At just about the same time that he disappeared inside, my reins got caught on a tree and were pulled out of my hands. Kola ran full speed into the garage after the mustang.

The garage had open overhead doors on both ends, so this was by no means the end of the trail for the mustang. I realized that this roundup was just beginning. Retrieving the reins, I began a ten- to fifteen-minute adventure that involved just about every kind of obstacle you could imagine, including wooden fences, barbed wire fences, and split rail fences. Luckily, I didn't have to jump those fences because the mustang had already gone through them, clearing a path for me. After half a dozen near-death experiences for both Kola and myself, the mustang managed to find its way into a pasture with some sheep in it and finally stopped. Someone showed up with a bucket of feed and after about an hour, we managed to get a halter on the runaway and call a veterinarian.

(continued on next page)

While walking Kola back home over the same route we had traveled an hour earlier, I reviewed all the obstacles we had negotiated. We were running on instinct with no time to consciously make the right maneuvers. Nevertheless, Kola understood my natural tendencies to lean toward and focus on the direction in which I wanted to go. He also carried out focal commands. I began to realize how much communication had taken place between Kola and me. Then I remembered the concept the Cheyenne woman had tried to explain to me two years earlier. She pointed out how birds, fish, and horses in a group

(continued at right)

Whenever we make an attempt to understand or comprehend something we focus on it. If we don't understand a shape or object we focus visually. If we don't understand a concept we focus mentally. This response to the need to understand can happen very quickly and is usually taken care of by our subconscious mind. When walking through the woods in unfamiliar territory, our subconscious mind looks at and focuses both visually and mentally on the place where we are about to place our feet. Once this spot has been identified and understood, our subconscious mind allows us to place our foot there. The feelers we send out are not entirely invisible, especially to animals who can sense what it is we are focusing on.

Another way we use focus is to try to convey a message to someone or something else. Herd animals are experts at this, possessing the ability to sense or know what the other members are focusing on. Although part of this awareness may be visual, a larger part of it is mental.

Focus is used along with physical or verbal cues and is what controls or initiates physical messages. Lean slightly forward, as if to increase speed, and focus on a point somewhere ahead of where you are at that moment. Practice developing subtle awareness of a point in front of you until you are able to recognize and utilize this powerful tool.

Horses know what you are concentrating on. To prove this, try the following test. Mount your horse and sit on his or her back in a very relaxed manner. Look at your horse and, without moving your body, say in your head "Do something!" Think this command very intensely as if there were something specific you wanted your horse to do, but do not concentrate on any one task. You will usually see immediate results such as an ear swiveling back toward you or your horse may even take a step or two on his own. By pointing an ear in your direction, your horse is saying, "I sense that you want me to do something, but without physical reinforcement, I don't know what it is." By taking a tentative step, your horse is trying something out in the form of a question: "Did you want me to go this way?"

If you want to turn left, but are focusing on something on your right, your horse may hesitate because your focal and physical cues are in conflict. However, if your focal and physical cues are in harmony, your horse's performance can be nothing short of beautiful. This is illustrated clearly by Olympic-level musical freestyle dressage riders. Native horsemen

know how to move or change direction at exactly the same time. It is because every member of the flock, school, or herd is aware of what the leader is focusing on. Focus is what allows a herd to perform its primary function, which is to act as one unit. The purpose of the herd is to be and act as a whole. A single unit composed of many is intimidating and confusing to predators. By becoming "one with" the others, each individual enjoys the safety that comes from being a part of a larger whole. Kola and I had previously established our own herd of two, and the dynamic we had developed paid off when I really needed it to.

would have been very proud of and impressed by the harmony that exists between those riders' physical and focal cues. Native American horsemen had no option but to focus on what they wanted their horses to do next. When riding amid a herd of bison that was sometimes thousands strong, there was no time to think about commands, body movements, or verbal requests. Nor was there time to memorize subtle and complicated sets of physical aids. Those buffalo hunters relied both on their horses' ability to sense what their riders wanted to do, and their horses' knowledge of the safest and most efficient way to do it.

Without focus, you may be sending mixed messages to your horse. If what you want your horse to do is not important enough to focus on, your horse may feel that it is not important enough to do.

The Bit

If there is one training tool that has been abused more than any other, it is the bit. Notice the bit is described here as a training tool and not a piece of riding equipment. Under the best circumstances, within which a healthy working relationship exists, the bit is used most effectively to reinforce verbal, physical, or focal cues.

You've probably heard that when you are on a horse's back, you are always training the horse, either positively or negatively. The vast majority of horses do whatever they can get away with. By consistently reinforcing your cues with a bit, you have the ability to augment them and leave no room for miscommunication. This does not mean you should inflict pain by tugging on your horse's mouth. It has become commonplace to increase the severity of a bit as the horse stops responding to the rider. The primary reason riders go to harsher bits and begin treating the bit as a tool of reprimand is that riders do not have or are not willing to devote time to healthy working relationships with their horses.

Almost all horses—95 percent of them—can be ridden successfully with a thick loose-ring snaffle bit (three-inch rings). It is amazing how quickly a horse is willing to forget about that double-twist, studded war bridle that he was becoming accustomed to. Contrary to popular belief, war bridles were not developed by Native Americans. The war bridles used in North America were used primarily by Spaniards, and only later by Native Americans.

A mild snaffle encourages the horse to look elsewhere to take its cues. Remember that the horse is a herd animal and its nature is to take cues from the itancan of its herd. If those cues become more and more subtle in one area, the horse is forced (by its nature) to pay attention to other areas in order to follow the itancan. Traditionally, Native American horseman used a thong, a "bit" that is nothing more than a braided piece of leather or rawhide that goes over the tongue and is tied or cinched under the horse's chin. A single rein extends up the left side of the horse's neck. Ideally, every horse should be comfortable with such a simple mouthpiece but realistically, this is not always possible—some horses need more direction and reassurance than others. Some horses do not trust themselves enough to have their riders' cues reinforced by only a piece of rawhide; some riders do not trust themselves enough to give those cues effectively with just a piece of rawhide. If either of these categories fits your situation, just remember that a horse's mouth is very sensitive. Do not abuse the bit. Throughout Relationship Training, view the bit as a cue-reinforcing training tool.

The hackamore is usually a less severe piece of equipment than the bit, and like the bit it is used to convey messages to your horse. Although a hackamore may be less likely than a bit to inflict pain, riding cues need not (and should not) be given by applying pressure to the nerves on the bridge of a horse's nose. This is an exceedingly sensitive area of the horse's face. Severe and ill-fitted hackamores can actually cut off the air passing through the horse's nostrils.

There are humane ways to use any bit or hackamore. If you feel only a hackamore will work, try a bosal, which uses similar principles but leaves less room for errors of fit and application. When using a bosal, don't get into a muscle contest with your horse by physically turning his head with the reins—you will lose. Like the ring snaffle, the bosal is ideally a tool used to reinforce your physical or focal cues.

Reins

Reins, like the bit, are also ideally used to reinforce your physical and focal cues. Traditionally, one rein was used by Native American horsemen. Some suggest that riding with no reins is the ultimate measure of a good rider, however this is impractical and does not provide the horse with enough reinforcement or confidence. When you start Relationship Training with your horse, apply the "direct-rein" method of using one rein aid at a time to guide your horse's head for turning, rather than the "neck-rein" method of holding both reins in one hand. It is less confusing to the horse to receive a single message, such as "turn," through his mouth than it is for him to receive a single message through both his mouth and his neck. Apply as little pressure as possible. When the horse is not understanding your commands, don't pull the reins harder. Instead, overemphasize your physical and focal cues, then repeat the command with the same rein pressure. This will teach your horse that communication will come from means other than through the mouth. The horse will soften focus on the bit and sharpen focus on your focal cues.

Don't ever use the bight, the loose-hanging ends of the reins, to slap your horse. Nor should the bight be used to inflict pain, even if the "pain" we're talking about is fairly insignificant. If it is necessary to give your horse a sharper physical cue in the early stages, use your hand and use it in a reassuring way. Although it is true a horse will usually move away from and in the opposite direction of the source of a stimulus (crop, reins, etc.), slapping the horse with the reins does not serve the ultimate goal of building a healthy working relationship.

I have worked extensively with horses training them one-on-one. I no longer do this, however, because Relationship Training must be used and learned by both horse and owner. The nuances of what passes between me and the horse don't do that horse any good when I leave, unless his or her owner applies the same approach. When I leave, I want the owner to be able to further the horse's training. Therefore, I insist that whenever possible, my clients attend their horses' sessions with me.

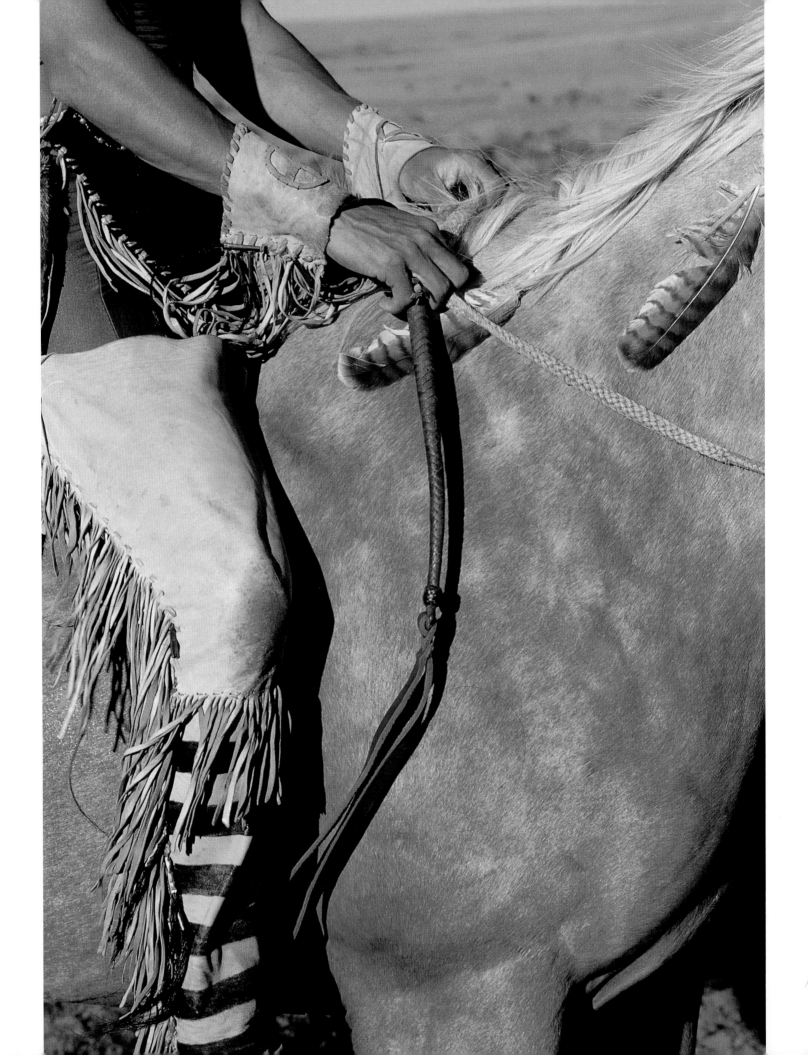

The Switch

The switch, a braided leather short whip about two feet long, was commonly used by Native American riders as a training tool. The switch was used more as a pat on the back than as a whip or instrument of pain. Used in this manner, the switch reinforces verbal, physical, and focal cues and can be a good training tool, especially in the beginning phases of training. The only problem with the switch is that if you do not practice self-control, it can become a way of administering punishment; your horse will come to view it more as a spanking tool than a training tool. Imagine that every time you got angry with your horse, you removed your hat and beat him with it. Your horse would soon begin to fear your hat (not you) and would act differently every time that punishment tool was sitting upon your head. The switch should be used to coax, not to tell.

Anticipation

There are crucial moments in Relationship Training when your horse begins to anticipate your requests. Look for them and learn to recognize them. Don't chat with friends or invite them to watch you as you work because it is very easy to miss these brief moments of anticipation. Here's an example of a way to develop your awareness for them.

Riding bareback and starting at a walk, center and balance your body so you and your horse are comfortable, meaning that you both move with ease and relaxed energy, and your horse is paying attention to you. To halt, pull up your knees about six inches so they are resting just behind your horse's shoulder blades. As you do this, lean back from your hips and allow your backward motion to slowly bring the reins back with you. Do not flex your arms—keep them in the same position. Allow the change in your torso to ease the reins back. Pay close attention to your horse's gait while doing this. At the instant that you feel a slight hesitation in his walk, drop your knees, sit up, and allow the reins to come forward again. Then, repeat the exercise.

As your horse begins to anticipate your request to slow down at the moment when you raise your knees, raise them once or twice and bring your horse to a complete stop before relaxing your aids—your knees, the reins, a shift in weight. After very little time, your horse should begin to anticipate your desire to halt. From this time forward, by raising your knees and leaning back slightly, you will effectively communicate the concept of halt.

After your horse understands the physical cues of you shifting your weight and adjusting your knees, you can use incrementally less pressure on your reins to reinforce your other cues. In this way, you make use of anticipation, a very important tool in every phase of training.

Anticipation can either cultivate focus or destroy it. This is why it's important to understand the type of anticipation to use. In many riding disciplines, anticipation is discouraged in horses because it keeps them from focusing on their riders. You can see negative anticipation when a horse is drilled, rather than guided, during riding. He begins to perform his movements by rote. He knows what comes next, and he's bored with the routine. He does not focus on his rider and is not tuned in for the next request. Positive anticipation, however, is your horse's ability to expect or await your requests. This has the opposite effect of negative anticipation in that it sharpens your horse's focus on you. The object of developing this tool is to cut down the amount of time between request and response so that the desired movement takes place nearly instantly. If you miss those crucial moments of anticipation, you will miss what Relationship Training is all about.

Timing is crucial in the training process. If you do not recognize that your horse is anticipating your request, you are not taking advantage of your horse's peak learning opportunities. When your horse is anticipating, he is understanding. When he is understanding, learning takes place more freely. Failing to encourage and reward your horse at the time he makes an effort to understand or carry out your requests, is like praising a child's A on her report card two weeks after she brings it home.

Praise

"Don't spoil your horse."

"You're going to ruin him."

"She'll turn into a pet."

"The horse can't concentrate if he knows you've got a pocket full of carrots."

These are all comments often heard by riders who frequently reward their horses for understanding requests correctly. Native American elders teach that when someone does a good thing, he or she should be rewarded. Our horses are no exception. Treats, pats, hugs, and kind words are regular parts of Relationship Training sessions. They are not given out every time a horse does what you ask. However, a horse who is trying very hard to understand your communication should be recognized.

It is possible for a horse to become spoiled. Avoid resorting to hugs and treats as bribes. But tuck a few treats into your pocket, and when you find yourself saying to your horse, "You did a great job—I wish there was some way I could show you my appreciation," reach into your pocket.

Saddles, Bareback, and Balance

Riders in all disciplines should ride bareback for at least two to three months. Bareback training is especially beneficial in the beginning stages of Relationship Training. Once a healthy working relationship has been established, riding with a saddle is perfectly satisfactory and probably more practical for most riders.

Work with a saddle that is as "close contact" as possible, meaning it has the least interference between you and your horse. Bulky billets, cumbersome trees, and lots of thick leather only inhibit your signals to your horse. It's crucial that your saddle fit your horse properly. Ask a saddler, respected trainer, or your veterinarian to help you determine whether your saddle fits your horse, and keep in mind that as horses age, gain or lose weight, and build or lose muscle, their physiology affects saddle fit. Therefore, a saddle that fit your horse three years ago (or even last winter) may not fit so well now.

It is also important to understand that a rider's physical cues can be more subtle while riding bareback than in the saddle. You will have to make some adjustments. If your horse is accustomed to taking cues from leg pressure, you will have to develop your balance without applying the same type of leg pressure. Incidentally, when riding bareback, do not hang on with your legs. Keep your balance by adjusting your center.

Balance may be described differently by different riders, but it is basically the position in which you are least likely to fall off your horse. The best way I know to understand balance is to ride a horse bareback for two to three hours. When you are relaxed and supple, you can experience balance. If you have not achieved balance while riding bareback, you have not experienced balance. This is not to say that you are not a balanced rider, but without being physically in contact with your horse, it is very hard to achieve true balance.

Balance learned in a saddle is closer to catching your balance than truly achieving balance. A saddle sits one to four inches above the horse's back. By raising your center of gravity even that small amount, it is much more difficult to stay on the horse's back. Pommels, cantles, stirrups, knee rolls and horns are there to help you catch your balance after it has been thrown off.

Your goal in riding bareback is to center yourself. You are centered when you draw your energy to a point just below your navel, making your abdomen and seat heavier than your upper body, relaxing your body and becoming balanced. By learning balance without the aid of the saddle, and by lowering your physical center as much as possible toward the horse, you can learn to balance and center your body much more quickly and more effectively.

When riding bareback, don't use a bareback pad. A bareback pad is an English-saddle-shaped piece of fleece or wool with a girth, usually made of nylon webbing. Some of them have handles at the pommel; some even have stirrups. People buy bareback pads for several reasons—to keep themselves from getting dirty, to provide some cushion to the rider or the horse, or because they think it will offer some stability. However, bareback pads can be extremely dangerous because they slide around as you ride, taking your focus off your horse and putting it on the pad. If you should grab the pad or handle in an attempt to regain your balance, you will find yourself hanging upside down under your horse. If you use a pad with stirrups and attempt to stand in them, you might as well stand on the ground because that is where you are going to end up. Any dirt and scurf you might get on your pants from your horse while riding bareback is unimportant when you recognize the benefits of being physically connected to him, without the danger and interference of a slippery piece of fabric between you.

. . . . . we are after all
a mere part of Creation . . . .
And we stand between
the mountain and the ant,
somewhere and only there,
as part
and parcel
of the
Creation.

—OREN R. LYONS, ONONDAGA

The tools of Relationship Training are just that, tools. They can be used to create, repair, adjust, or improve any part of the relationship that we are nurturing. If we can become comfortable with the tools and use them in a manner that is consistent with our understanding of the horse, our efforts will be clearly rewarded. With the aid of these tools, our goal of harmony within the herd, our two member herd, can be achieved.

If your concern is that Creator has not given you ample padding to ride a horse without some sort of saddle or pad, rest assured. I have completed more than a few twenty- to thirty-mile rides without the aid of a saddle or even a pad. I have also done twenty- to thirty-mile rides with a saddle, and one with a bareback pad. When I ride bareback, I am usually the one back at camp who can still walk after the ride, who doesn't have sores or blisters, and who doesn't worry about staying warm during cold-morning rides.

3

Exercises for Relationship Training

The following exercises can help you build a stronger relationship with your horse. All are intended to be done (and are most beneficial when done) while riding bareback. A few of these exercises have been modified, but most of them remain as they were taught from generation to generation by Native American horsemen.

Time is a critical element in this, the first and most important exercise. Relationship Training is all about getting to know your horse so you can communicate with him. If your communication is to be two way, you'll need to know how to receive messages from your horse, and to do that, you'll need to understand your horse.

At one point, I faced a training stale-mate with one of my horses who had become erratic in his responses to my requests. The horse seemed moody and inconsistent. I consulted an elderly Native American gentleman to help me identify and solve the problem. Understand that Native American elders frequently answer a question with a question, hoping that you will find your own answer. He asked me, "Which grass in the pasture is your horse's favorite? Which foot does he lead with when traveling downhill? How many times does he nap during the day? Does your horse enjoy the company of any certain birds during the day?"

As you can guess, my answer to all of his questions was, "I don't

(continued at right)

EXERCISE ONE

. . . .

Spend a Day with Your Horse

SPENDING A DAY WITH YOUR HORSE MAY BE THE MOST IMPORTANT learning tool in this or any other book concerning horses. It can be performed by a novice or an expert and requires no special talents or skills to achieve dramatic results.

This is one of the most profoundly simple exercises in this book, yet it can be the most rewarding. When you do this exercise, free your schedule and your mind of other pressures, plans, and problems. Get up just before dawn and go to see your horse. If he's in a stall at night, enter the barn and find a comfortable place to observe him quietly. If he's kept in a pasture all night, enter the pasture and position yourself so that you don't draw too much attention. The horses in the barn and pasture will likely notice a human in their quarters and may expect you to feed them. But remain quiet and unobtrusive. Do not talk to or pat your horse or the others. You are there to observe. Feed your horse at his regular time, or if someone else feeds the horses, allow him or her to do so without help or interference from you. Become an element of your horse's surroundings as best you can.

Pay attention to what your horse is doing and why. Take notes on your horse's actions and motivations. There are thousands of questions to which you can find answers simply by passively observing your horse. Who in your horse's herd is he closest to? Are there any members of the herd that he has petty grievances with? How does he resolve them—does he get in squabbles or does he normally back down? Does he initiate physical contact, either positive or negative? Is he patient with the intrusive behavior of his herdmates? How does he respond to a herd member's request for mutual grooming or fly-swatting?

Is he a picky eater, choosing only the best grass from each section of the pasture, or does he "sweep" an entire area? Where is his favorite place to nap? Does he stay with the herd, or does he venture off by himself (or with a friend)? Does he vocalize more or less than his herdmates? When and why does he vocalize? Does he watch as the others get a good gallop going? Does he initiate a herd gallop? Does he participate at all or simply watch? Is he more sensitive to his surroundings than his pasturemates, swiveling his

ears, stopping his grazing to look around, and continuing to look at distur-bances long after the rest of the horses have returned to grazing?

What is his reaction to people who come up to the fence or enter the pasture, to horses on the other side of the fence, or to dogs? Does he ignore them? For how long? Does he approach them in a friendly way? Does he approach them in a territorial way? When other people remove horses from the pasture, does your horse tag along? Try to follow? Harass the horse who's being led? Harass the person for treats or attention? Does your horse play in the water trough, chew on tree branches or fence boards, paw the dirt, shake his head a lot, or scratch himself on fence posts?

Do his eyes run when he's either inside or outside? Does his nose run? Does the consistency of his manure change? How much does he drink? What sweating or shedding patterns can you observe? How many times in a day does he roll? Where and how does he roll? Does he roll only when other horses are far away from him?

This is only a sampling of the questions you could answer by spending a single day observing your horse. If you did this exercise regularly, you'd see that some of the answers even change with your horse's moods, hormonal cycles, physical condition, and the seasons.

Get to know your horse as well as you possibly can. By learning what motivates your horse's actions, you can begin to understand the best way to communicate your requests. Horses are individuals, and unless we understand the individual we cannot expect the individual to understand us.

know," to which he answered, "Spend a day with your horse." I did.

I observed that my horse shied away whenever other horses approached him on his right side. It was clear he was protecting something on that side of his body. Later, after examining him more closely back in his stall, I confirmed that something was the matter with his hip. If I hadn't observed him in pas-ture, in the company of other horses, his hip condition would not have made itself apparent until it became severe. Even the veterinarian hadn't detected the problem.

I have since spent many days following my horse around the pasture, observing his daily habits, becoming familiar with who he is.

Introducing Tools

IT IS IMPORTANT THAT YOUR HORSE BE 100 PERCENT COMFORTABLE WITH the tools you use to communicate with him. A tool is anything used during training or riding that your horse does not usually encounter when he is at liberty. Tools include you, along with your voice, weight, movements, and hands.

This exercise should be used any time a new tool is introduced to your horse. The goal is to have your horse view these objects as part of his everyday existence. It is also important that your horse understand that these tools are used when there is a particular task to be completed. The training process is virtually the same, no matter which tool is being introduced.

The first tool to introduce to your horse is your hands. You need to be able to touch and manipulate every part of your horse's body with your hands. Run your hands all over your horse's body as if you were brushing him. Pay close attention to your horse's reactions. You may find several areas that make your horse uncomfortable. These sensitive or ticklish spots are the areas in which you must gain his confidence. The cause of these sensitive areas can vary from chiropractic problems to scars to bad or good experiences that have conditioned your horse to identify certain areas of his body with certain reactions. For example, a horse who's been handled roughly or hit on the face and head may be defensive when your hands approach his head; and a horse who has enjoyed close physical interaction with his pasturemates may display affection and enjoyment when your hands pass over his withers and mane or crest. Some horses are exceedingly sensitive. Many are ticklish around their bellies and flanks.

Once these sensitive areas have been identified, focus on them. If you discover that your horse is not comfortable with his ears being touched, use slow, deliberate, firm movements to gain his trust in this matter. Rub his ears firmly, but do not grab or squeeze them. Watch his reaction. When he seems to be saying, "I don't like this" (by increasing his aversion to your hands), move immediately down his neck and continue stroking. Go back

up to his ears several times and stop immediately when his tolerance level tops out again. Keep your actions quiet and supportive. The object is not to subdue your horse. Keep your touches soft and firm so you don't tickle him. Don't squeeze or press hard; just make and keep contact. Each time you do this, your horse's tolerance will increase.

There is an important moment in this exercise that you should watch for carefully. At some point, your horse will act as if to say, "That's enough of the ear thing!" It may be a throw of the head or a step backward. These acts of retreat usually mean, "I get your point, but I still don't feel wholly comfortable with my ears being touched." At this point, give the ears one more stroke, then move down your horse's neck. You will usually find that each time you do the "ear thing," your horse's tolerance will grow greater until there is no longer a problem with you touching his ears.

Once your horse is totally comfortable with your hands on all parts of his body, you can do the same with all the tools you will be using. The switch should be the next tool you familiarize your horse with. Use this exercise even if you've been riding with a crop for years. Touch or brush your horse all over with the switch, watching again for sensitive areas and making adjustments to his comfort level. If the areas sensitive to the switch are the same that were sensitive to your hands, go back over these areas with your hands. If you discover new areas of discomfort—usually the rump or neck because this may be where a crop was used as punishment in the past—work on them in the same way that you did with your hands, watching all the while for feedback from your horse. Holding the switch with the popper, or "business end," pointing down works best. This point-down position eliminates the possibility of your horse thinking that you are raising it as if to strike him.

After your horse has shown you he is comfortable with the switch, move on to the headstall, bit, blanket, and every other tool you ask your horse to accept. Allow your horse to smell, lick, or even chew on any of the tools. Horses are tactile animals and investigate things and situations with their muzzles and mouths.

When your horse has become almost bored with all the tools and accepts them as commonplace, you are ready to move on. This exercise is not an ongoing process for the life of your relationship—once the horse is comfortable and trusts you, there should be no reason to go over it again. However, this exercise can and should be reinforced if ever your horse appears to be intimidated or scared of a particular tool. The most convenient time to reinforce this exercise is at feeding time. Give your horse a physical once-over with any of the tools you will be using, or even with your hands if he is exhibiting signs of insecurity in the relationship.

WHEN DOING THIS EXERCISE, NATIVE AMERICANS USUALLY HELD A PIECE of cloth or leather in one hand. The cloth served as a focal point for the horse and defined where he should devote his attention. As you work on this exercise, hold a cloth in one hand. Don't wave it around or touch your horse with it—simply have it with you. The role played by the cloth in this exercise is simply to get the horse to associate it with opportunities to communicate with you, learn, and receive praise. It serves the same purpose as a uniform or a desk. Your horse will become accustomed to seeing it in his field of vision and will associate it with a lesson. He will come to attention when he sees it. This is not to say that you will never have his attention and cooperation unless you have the training cloth—your relationship with your horse is what develops the cooperation and connection you're seeking. But the cloth, and your horse's association with it, will help put your horse in the right frame of mind because he will know that you and he are about to work on something that requires his focus.

Start this exercise by leading your horse. An eight-foot lead works best. Face your horse, holding the lead by the end. Position your hand about a foot from your horse's nose and level with where the lead connects to the halter. This position gives you room for three to four backward steps before the lead becomes taut. It gives the horse a chance to understand what you want him to do before you get to the point that you would be pulling on the halter. Your mind-set should not be that of pulling (asking or telling) but of leading (by example).

As you walk backward, make soft eye contact with your horse, encouraging him without words, and watch his movements. Praise him the instant he takes a step toward you to follow. Give him a moment to make the connection between what just transpired and the reward, then do the exercise again. Most horses will begin following you with your first step after only a few tries.

The next step in this exercise is to teach your horse to stop after he has begun following you. Take the lead rope, face your horse, and begin walking backward as before. As your horse follows, walk a few more steps and then stop abruptly. As soon as your horse hesitates or begins to stop, walk forward and reward him with a pat or kind word. Do this several times, each time rewarding him for following your lead. Do the same exercises again, this time asking your horse to sidestep. Follow the same reward sequence.

After your horse seems to get the hang of following—when his responses are immediate and consistent—do the exercise from a walk rather than a halt. Rewarding your horse's responses immediately helps him understand which part of the exercise he is being rewarded for. In the beginning, it is important to maintain eye contact with your horse, but after a short while, you will be able to do this exercise walking forward at your horse's side, rather than backward and positioned in front of him.

Now that your horse is shadowing your movements, teach him when to shadow and when not to. He will learn primarily by your body language. From a halt, back away from your horse slowly. Change your focus from coaxing body language and attitude to a distancing manner, as if you were mentally holding your horse at arm's length. Concentrate on the horse's front feet and imagine the feet and legs as cement pillars set in the ground. Do not make eye contact. Clench the cloth in an unmoving fist. When your horse begins to follow, take a step toward him to ask him to stop, but do not reward him with the usual praise. If he begins to follow but then hesitates, step forward and reward him. Each time you step away from your horse, count how many seconds go by before your horse moves forward. The object is to increase the time that your horse will stand without moving until told to do otherwise.

Avoid vocal commands at this point; they will confuse matters later when you begin mounted work. Your horse will soon learn by your physical cues, or body language, what it is you are trying to communicate. By focusing on certain images such as movement or standing still, you are conveying certain messages that come naturally. Horses can read this body language even though you are probably unaware of all the cues you are giving. For example, when you are asking your horse to stand until told to do otherwise, you avoid eye contact, clench the cloth, and focus—envision that the horse has cement legs. But there are other signals you give. You are probably standing with your feet together, your teeth are probably slightly clenched, your shoulders are squared, and you are frowning. This body language occurs naturally when humans nonverbally communicate the thought, "don't move." These signals will happen automatically, however, don't try to act them out.

Although this exercise is not physically demanding, it requires a lot of concentration on the part of both participants, the two- and the four-legged. Be reasonable in your expectations. Do not ask your horse to stand and stare at you for forty-five minutes, although after three or four years of work together, you should be able to do this. Work on this exercise only as long as your horse's attention span allows. The attention span of your horse will increase every time you do this exercise. Once your horse understands how to follow your lead, take your horse through a number of fun, follow-the-leader sessions. It's a good idea to start with this exercise as a refresher course when teaching your horse something new.

EXERCISE FOUR

· ·

Getting On

GETTING ON A HORSE SHOULD BE AN EASY, FLUID MOTION THAT DOES not compromise the balance of the horse or rider. Without the aid of stirrups, mounting becomes somewhat of a gymnastic exercise but with the proper technique can be a swift and graceful task. Jumping up and resting your belly on the horse, then swinging your legs over the horse is not an ideal way of mounting your horse. The movement is not fluid, and it includes a moment of vulnerability and loss of balance for both you and the horse. Here's a better way.

Stand next to your horse facing the opposite direction. Your shoulder should be six to eight inches from your horse's withers, and if you're mounting from the left, position your left foot about four inches from your horse's front left hoof. Support all your weight on your left leg and swing your right leg once or twice without it touching the ground. Place your left hand on the back of your horse's withers in a tent shape—your fingers on your horse's right side and your thumb on his left. Hold your reins in your left hand.

Swing your right leg back about three feet away from your left foot, then bring it forward and up toward the horse's back. Keep your left leg planted until the momentum of your right leg brings it up off the ground. The goal is to swing your right leg up and over your horse's back so that the back of your right knee lands on the right-hand side of the horse's back, at about the middle of his back. Keep your right leg fairly straight as you swing it up—too much bend in your knee will cause your foot to get hung up on the left side of your horse. When your right knee has reached its target on the horse's back, to the right of his spine, extend your right leg downward, shifting your weight to an imaginary right stirrup. This will turn your body so that you are facing the same direction as your horse and your left leg will be lifted by your momentum.

Keep your left hand stationary during mounting. It is not used to pull you up, but rather to steady your efforts. To illustrate the role of your left hand, try this exercise. Stand about arm's length from a wall and raise one foot without touching the wall. See how long you can stand on one foot without losing your balance. Now try it again, this time with one finger touching the wall. You will be able to stand on one foot without falling out of balance until your supporting leg gets tired. That one finger is all it takes to help you maintain your balance because it gives you a steady frame of reference from

which the rest of your body can balance itself. During mounting, your left hand serves the same purpose—to give you a solid reference point.

At the same time that your right knee makes contact with your horse, your right forearm should be placed on the right side of the horse's withers. Because you have planted your right knee and right forearm simultaneously, you will be lying on your belly facing forward. Your head should end up on the right side of the horse's neck. Bend your right arm at a ninety-degree angle and sweep it from right to left as you extend your right leg toward your imaginary stirrup, and sit up straight. This will put you in the riding position.

Practice this exercise a few times on a quiet mount, with a friend holding the horse's lead. Accustom your horse to this exercise in stages. Place your forearm over his withers and over his back. Swing your right leg so that he gets used to your movements. Make several starts and praise him when he stands still for you. Ask a friend to hold his lead when you mount completely for the first time.

EXERCISE FIVE

Using Focus in the Saddle

NOW THAT YOUR HORSE IS COMPLETELY COMFORTABLE WITH YOU AND your tools and can follow your lead to your satisfaction, it's time to climb aboard and put your focal cues to use in the saddle. In this exercise, you'll wean yourself from your reliance on physical aids and learn to trust your focal form of communication by using only focus to direct your horse. Inexperienced Native American riders were required to do this exercise without the aid of reins or a cinch (mouthpiece) and were not permitted to speak to their horses. This is much more challenging to the rider than it is to the horse.

This is the point at which most riders begin to break down the lines of communication that were established in the previous exercises because they are now in an uncomfortable situation. Humans are most at ease on their own two feet. No matter how experienced we may be as riders, we will never be as comfortable on the back of a horse as we are when standing on the ground. We cannot devote the same amount of energy to communication with our horses while riding as we do during ground exercises because a certain amount of energy is being used to stay balanced and secure.

You'll have to establish your bareback seat, the position while mounted bareback in which you are comfortable, confident, balanced, and effective. When at a walk, your shoulders should be square over your hips, your back relaxed and straight, and your chest open (not slouching with a rounded back). Your hips should absorb and follow the motion of the horse, your midsection—between your hips and ribcage—should be fluid in motion, and your shoulders relaxed and relatively still so that your upper body is not rocking around as your horse walks. You will find a slot behind your horse's shoulder blades in which your leg fits as though it were meant to be there.

If your leg doesn't fall immediately into this slot, position yourself more toward the horse's withers. The best way to get a feel for this leg slot is to walk your horse down a steep slope while riding bareback. Lean back and stand up in your imaginary stirrups while pointing your toes down. Your legs will fit behind a natural set of "knee rolls" formed by your horse's shoulder muscles. This slot is where your legs should be for most maneuvers while riding bareback. After you can recognize and use this slot, you will find it easy to post while trotting.

Once on your horse's back, relax and watch signs that your horse is focusing on you: one or both ears swivel back toward you, he stands quietly, waiting for communication from you, and he is not calling to or giving all his attention to his herdmates or wandering around the ring, paddock, or arena in a distracted way. Be quiet and balanced on his back and communicate using the same signals you used when you were on the ground. Focus on a specific spot in the ring where you would like to go. Rely solely on the

There are times when you may have to stray from *Relationship Training* in the beginning stages, but do not stray for long.

My other horse Mihunka is a gem. He is a three-year-old gelding who has not yet learned bad habits or behaviors. The fact that he has been trained in the way I consider to be correct from the beginning makes him very delicate. I don't want to teach him things that I consider to be wrong out of my own haste or irresponsibility.

When I felt he was ready, I took him on a short trail ride with some friends. About an hour into the ride, we encountered a deep stream. Mihunka clearly did not like the idea of cold water up to his chest. After ten minutes of dancing around, Mihunka decided to jump from one bank to the other. He did not clear the water, banged his right front hoof on a sizable rock, and spooked. At first, I couldn't get him to stop. Even though he had begun learning to stop with light pressure applied to a rope halter,

(continued at right)

focal commands that you gave your horse while on the ground. If you notice that you tend to lean forward slightly when trying to direct your horse to move forward, that's okay; when you focus, your natural tendency to shift your center in the direction in which you want to go is a reaction to concentrating on moving forward. Do not overemphasize the physical command of leaning, making it the primary method by which you communicate with your horse. If your horse should take half a step in the direction that you are focusing on without responding to any previously learned physical cues, reward him immediately and generously. This is definitely a moment in which treats are in order, so keep them on hand.

This exercise can be extremely frustrating if done incorrectly. It is difficult to lead a horse while seated behind his head and out of his field of vision. People today are taught to ride in a linear way, with specific directions for what to do with each part of their body. Focal riding requires that we use the intangibles of instinct, concentration, and intuition. You must sharpen your intangible skills in Relationship Training, and the results will be well worth the effort to realign your whole approach.

Practice by leading your horse while on the ground just as you did in the previous exercise. Focus on where you want to go, not the place that you want your horse to go. It is your job to lead—not to tell—your horse to follow. If you get on your horse's back and can't remember what you were thinking when you were leading the horse on the ground, return to the ground and pay extra attention to the mental and focal cues that you are giving. The most important part of this exercise is that you not return to training by telling—do everything possible to avoid falling back into old habits.

When you achieve success with the exercise, do it several more times to reinforce it. You will notice that your horse's responses get quicker and more consistent when a successful exercise is repeated. Do not overdo it, however. Some riders get so elated by their success with this exercise of using nonverbal, nonphysical communication that they do it over and over and quickly teach their horses that this chore of focal communication is boring. Keep in mind that the reward being offered is given for your horse's ability to decipher your focal communications, not for doing what he was told. This feeling of gratitude will be reflected in your tone and body language if it is sincere.

The ability to communicate focally does not come quickly or easily and requires constant attention. It will become easier and more natural as time goes on, but remember, all it takes is one two-hour trail ride using old habits and techniques to destroy the lines of communication that you have established. There will be exceptions—for instance, when your horse spooks or tries to turn for home. If you need to use the old ways to regain control momentarily, do so. Once you have regained control, however, go back to the methods of Relationship Training.

Once your horse can decipher your focal cues, try to lead him through some basic maneuvers—halt, walk, turn—then move on to more refined maneuvers, such as asking for only a few steps at a time. If you are paying attention to your horse's communications, you will know when he is ready to move on to more challenging tasks.

If a physical cue, such as a shift in balance, starts to emerge in any one of the basic directions, use it; but do not rely on it to communicate. Your body will act on its own to follow what you are focusing on. If you focus on turning left, for instance, you will turn your head to the left. Don't expect your horse to turn left because you turned your head to the left, though. These physical reinforcements are merely secondary actions that occur naturally. Don't analyze them, memorize them, or try to replicate them as aids.

I had no choice but to pull back as hard as I could on the left rein to spin him around. This was clearly not part of any of our previous training sessions, and after he settled down a bit, I had a decision to make. Should I continue the ride and possibly face more spooky situations, hoping that he would become numb to them, or should I cut my losses and work with something he was more familiar with? Because I value the relationship between us more than immediate results, I chose the latter. I removed the training cloth from my pocket, replaced his bridle with a rope halter, and used a four-mile version of the leading exercise. During those four miles, we successfully crossed two more streams and did it in a much more constructive fashion than before.

The point is that if Mihunka lives a full life, and Creator permits, I will be riding him until I am fifty to sixty years old, and we will have a close relationship based on trust and communication.

Physical cues should be used only to reinforce focal cues. For example, when you ask your horse to move forward, you might assume that he does so because you sat up a little on the inside of your thighs and leaned forward a bit. Once your horse understands this exercise, however, his front foot will be on the move before you ever had the chance to change your center. If you focus on moving forward and do not reinforce the communication by changing your center, your horse will hesitate and raise his eyebrows, indicating confusion. He has learned to take cues from your focus, reinforced by your physical cues.

After mastering focal communication, you can bask in the fact that the five or six years of riding lessons usually needed to achieve this stage of communication will not be necessary. Mastering focal communication tends to happen after years of lessons, but it happens by accident. If you are taking lessons to learn to ride a horse, focal communication between you and the lesson horse happens inadvertently. However, if you plan to ride a certain horse—your horse—for any length of time, you will find much greater success by learning the basic elements of communication before attempting to have a conversation.

Incidentally, do not take the achievements of this exercise lightly. If successful, you are well on your way to developing a strong working relationship with your horse and perhaps will look at Dr. Dolittle in a different light from this point forward.

I learned about physical cues one hot summer in Oklahoma. My teacher was an elderly Kiowa gentleman who was a husband, father, grandfather, great-grandfather, singer (traditional southern drum), veteran, and part-time stand-up comedian at pow- wows. My usual response to his teachings was to laugh and scratch my head. The message in all his teachings was that if I wanted to learn how to communicate with a horse, the best place to start was by consulting my horse, not by asking a two-legged.

PHYSICAL CUES ARE MOST EFFECTIVE WHEN USED AS REINFORCEMENT tools. There is a place for all three types of communication, verbal, physical, and focal, when riding your horse. The most effective use of the physical cue is to back up any focal cues that you may be giving your horse. The most blatant misuse of the physical cue is kicking a horse to get him to move or to move faster. Kicking is a classic telling communication: "Move forward or I will kick you again" is the message. If you have made any headway with focal communication, you can begin to understand that kicking is not necessary.

Many trainers have a philosophy that horses move away from a heel or leg aid. It is common to hear instructors telling riders that if they want their horses to stay on the rail, they should apply pressure with the inside leg and the horse will move away from it. The problem with this approach is that you are not focusing on where you want to go. Rather, you are focusing on where you don't want your horse to go. Always direct or lead your horse toward something, rather than away from it.

If your horse does not respond to your focal cues or physical reinforcements, take the month or two necessary to implement and firmly establish the methods and exercises preceding this step.

When riding bareback, your lower leg naturally falls six to eight inches behind your horse's front leg. Your horse's center of gravity while on the move is located about halfway up your shin, four to six inches behind your calf. Your center of gravity while seated on your horse is just below your navel, about midway between your navel and your spine. When you ride, you create a combined center located approximately six inches below your horse's withers, depending on your weight. This combined center provides a sensitive steering mechanism. By leaning, you shift the combined center, which encourages your horse to realign and reestablish natural balance by moving under it. Even with the slightest movements, you can communicate to your horse where you would like to go.

(continued at right)

The best way I know to understand the concept of a combined center is to put yourself in your horse's position. Enlist the help of a forty- to eighty-pound child and carry him or her on your shoulders. This creates a combined center located somewhere near your sternum. Close your eyes and walk around, asking the child to steer you by leaning slightly in any direction. (I hesitate to use the word "lean" because this is not like leaning into a turn on horseback. When on your horse's back, it takes a movement of only a couple of inches to get a response).

If your horse does not respond at first to focal cues reinforced by subtle physical cues, it is usually because he has been conditioned to move when kicked. You'll have to do a bit of retraining.

Begin at a halt. Focus on the point where you would like to go and reinforce your focal cue by moving the combined center in that direction. When starting this exercise focus on a point somewhere about three miles ahead of you. In this way, there can be no mistake that the direction you want to go is forward. As soon as your horse responds—with a step, half-step, or even by shifting his weight in the right direction—reward him. If he walks in the direction you desire to go, let him take a few steps to reinforce the lesson, then ask him to stop.

After you and your horse can do a few successful stop and go sequences, do the exercise again, this time turning from a stop. Focus, change your combined center, and when your horse makes any move in the right direction, reward him immediately and generously. When he is confident enough to respond by turning from the halt, repeat the exercise once or twice more (don't drill the horse) and then reward him to reinforce the lesson.

The next step is to ask your horse to back up. This comes hardest to riders attempting to establish focal communication with their horses. Focusing on moving backward while facing forward can seem impossible in the beginning. All that is necessary to provide a good strong focal cue to move backward is to turn your head. It doesn't matter which way you turn it—right or left. Do whatever is most natural to you. Your body will adjust to maintain your balance. Focus on a point about three miles behind your horse and alter your combined center appropriately. When your horse makes any attempt to move backward—lifting a foot or shifting his weight by lowering his haunches and bringing his head toward his chest—reward him immediately and generously.

If you find that your horse is having a hard time getting used to these subtle cues, emphasize your physical cues to help him understand in a way he has become accustomed to. As your horse becomes more familiar with your commands, make them more and more subtle.

Once your horse grasps the concept of focal cues supported by subtle physical cues, start combining messages to your horse by doing this exercise on the move. From a halt, ask your horse for a turning walk. As he walks, praise him, then center yourself and focus on another turn. As he executes the turn, praise him again and ask for another. Ask for a halt, then back up a few steps. Walk again around the perimeter of the ring or arena (this asks him to wait for your cues), then ask for a few more turns. See if he'll do a circle for you, a figure eight, a change of direction on the rail, and step over a ground pole. Halt and back up again. By now, the communication between the two of you should be coming fairly easily, and your horse will gain confidence about how to do what you're asking.

When work in the walk is established, meaning that your horse responds correctly and consistently to your cues, you are ready to try it at the faster gaits. To ask for a trot, sit more firmly on your inner thighs, as if standing in stirrups. It may help to point your toes down.

A word of caution: Many riders undo much of the work done in these sessions without even realizing it. Say you and your horse can finally perform figure eights without any kicking or mouth-pulling from you, and in your delight, you yank your horse to a halt, dismount, and reward him. The reward is great, but your horse is probably thinking two things—one, "We're going back to the old tell-me-what-to-do-by-yanking-on-my-mouth routine," and two, "If I do something right, my rider will get off my back and I can go eat." Hugs, pats, and treats can be given while on your horse's back, and in this way, you will not send mixed messages.

You should understand almost immediately how easy it is for your horse to decipher subtle cues of shifting the combined center. When the child leans to the right, it is impossible not to understand in which direction your "rider" would like you to go. The same is true for your horse. The shift in combined center not only sends a clear message to your horse, but it also makes it very difficult for your horse to do anything but go in the direction you would like him to.

NOTE: Even though you grasped within a few seconds the communication that your horse receives from his rider, repeat this exercise often—it is good for the kid.

Remember, when you are the itancan of your two-member herd, you can do only one of two things at any given time. You can either enhance your relationship or diminish it. Take care to enhance it twice as much as you are inadvertently destroying it.

Exercise Seven

. . . .

Falling Off

THE FIRST THING TO UNDERSTAND ABOUT LEARNING TO FALL CORRECTLY is when to bail out and when to ride out the storm. If you have ever fallen off a horse, you are probably able to recognize the point at which your efforts to stay on became moot and falling was inevitable. This is the point of no return. Prior to the point of no return is when you must decide whether or not to bail. If you decide to bail out in a situation where you could have recovered, there is probably no harm done. If you wait too long in a dangerous situation, however, eventually the decision will no longer be yours.

As with mounting, the falling procedure is one fluid movement. Please practice this exercise with the help of a trainer or spotter. Although that person will not be around to help when you take a real fall, it is important to have someone there to help you in the beginning and evaluate your progress. The techniques for falling off are effective whether you ride with a saddle or not.

While still holding the reins, plant your forearms on either side of your horse's withers, which will bring your torso forward and over the withers. Release the reins. Lower your torso so that your belly is in contact with the horse, and kick both feet out of your stirrups and over the left side of the horse. If you are practicing this exercise bareback, imagine that you have stirrups; this will give you the proper feel of the exercise. In a single movement, after your feet are free of the stirrups, let the momentum of that backward kick send your legs over the horse's rump, supporting most of your weight on your forearms. When your legs are clear of your horse, push away from him with your arms by extending them, as if you were pushing someone away from you. Throw your body as far away from your horse and to the left as possible. This will make you airborne, facing your horse's hind end.

Do not try to break your fall by extending your arms or legs. Your momentum will carry you backward in the direction your horse is traveling. You will now do a backward roll, your body meeting the ground in the following order: left foot, left knee, left hand, left buttock, right hand and

buttock, both elbows. At this point, your legs should be crossed at the ankles and your knees bent at a ninety-degree angle. Stay as relaxed as possible as the momentum rolls you back.

It's very important that you release the reins before kicking your legs back. Your momentum will send your body in a clockwise direction, and most riders instinctively hang onto the reins with their left hand and try to break their fall with their right. This not only makes for a dangerous landing, but by pulling on the left rein, you could steer your horse right on top of you.

Practice landing before you mount by using this technique while falling backward from a standing position. Do this on a soft surface so you don't injure your spine, and wear safety equipment. Before practicing, whether on or off your horse, do some simple stretching exercises. The most important thing to remember about falling off is to relax. Rigid muscles prevent you from having full use of your body, and they get injured far more easily than relaxed ones.

The type of verbal cue you use is important when conveying either stop or go. You can use any word you like, but here are some pointers for deciding on which words to use.

Be sure the words you use as verbal cues are natural to you, ones you use already. In a situation where you have to make a quick stop, you don't want to have to rack your brain to remember your "stop" word. In fact, these cues do not have to be real words but can be mere vocables, such as the commands used by mule or draft horse drivers. The verbal cues will flow from you more naturally if they're already a comfortable fixture in your speech.

Make sure the words are different enough that your horse can decipher them. Horses are widely thought to perceive syllables and vowel sounds more clearly than anything else. With this in mind, do not make your stop and go cues "whoa" and "go." I use a word pronounced whee-chja for my "go" verbal command. This is a Comanche word that usually conveys celebration or excitement. For "stop," I use a word pronounced schkee, a Cherokee slang word that roughly translates to "thank you."

Using Verbal Cues

VERBAL COMMANDS ARE MOST EFFECTIVE WHEN DEFINING THE BEGINNING or end of a work session, or to communicate stop and go. Riders who use a lot of verbal commands in their riding are communicating with their horses as if they were humans. Limiting your verbal cues requires that you think like a horse. Humans think and communicate in verbal terms, whereas horses are physical and perceptive creatures. Trying to attach a verbal cue to every focal and physical communication only complicates things. When you focus on a direction and reinforce the focal cue by changing the combined center, there are more than enough communications being sent to convey your message. If you want to achieve a sliding stop or an out-of-the-gate start, however, verbal cues can be of great assistance. Both can be accomplished without the aid of verbal cues, but when starting out, make these nonverbal messages clear and concise.

When practicing your stop and go exercises with verbal cues, your switch can be especially helpful. It's also effective to have a bit of a pep talk with your horse before attempting a rapid start. Get your horse psyched up about the fact that you are about to jettison down the runway. This is sort of like revving up a dragster before you head down the quarter-mile. Your horse will hear the excitement in your voice, which is more meaningful to him than your words, and that will heighten his readiness for the next command. Perhaps you will give him a few pats on the neck, followed by some words in a higher pitch of voice. Why would you want to rev up your quiet, trustworthy horse? There are many situations, especially trail riding, when you want your horse to be prepared to move immediately to avoid a dangerous situation. If your ride requires you to deal with roads, railroad tracks, falling trees, rocks, or other riders, the ability to get your horse to respond quickly to your cues becomes a safety imperative.

Establish this response and cue recognition at home in the safety of the ring. When your horse can feel your excitement from the pep talk and is ready to take off, place the switch flat against the side of your horse's neck. In one gesture, give your verbal cue and sweep the switch from front to back until it hits your thigh. The switch should be on the right side of your horse's neck. Be careful not to catch the switch in your horse's mane.

If your horse moves forward even the slightest bit, reward him and do the exercise again. With practice, you will be able to take off without the switch. Your horse will begin to associate your verbal cue with your focal cue.

Stopping abruptly uses cues nearly opposite to those of taking off quickly. The primary difference is your focus. While trotting or cantering, pick a spot on the ground ahead and focus on it. Place the switch flat against your horse's rump, and in one movement change your combined center rearward by sitting up straighter, sweep the switch from back to front until it hits the back of your thigh, and give your verbal cue. If your horse hesitates in the slightest, reward him immediately. Don't be too concerned with stopping precisely at the spot you picked. You will soon discover how long it takes for your horse to stop, and therefore when you need to put on the brakes, so to speak.

Remember the rule of inertia: a body at rest tends to stay at rest. If you don't adjust your center forward before moving forward, especially at an energetic pace, you will slide off the back of your horse. By the same token, a body in motion tends to stay in motion, so if you do not adjust your center backward when stopping, especially when you stop abruptly, you will be thrust forward onto your horse's neck or over one shoulder.

If you are trying to achieve a sliding stop as seen in Western reining patterns, use leg wraps on your horse's legs. It takes only one good arena burn on your horse's fetlocks to convince him that sliding to a stop should not be attempted again.

Jumping

IF YOU RIDE ON TRAILS, JUMPING IS NECESSARY FROM TIME TO TIME. Jumping bareback can be a rewarding experience, but it can also be dangerous. If you have not jumped with a saddle or if you don't have any previous jumping training, do not attempt to jump bareback. If, on the other hand, you feel comfortable enough to try a few low jumps, wear a helmet and the other appropriate safety gear, and have someone present when you begin jumping bareback. Be sure you can perform all the preceding exercises at all gaits consistently and comfortably without a saddle before you attempt to jump bareback.

Modern riding instruction includes some good, sound, common-sense riding techniques in the area of jumping. Focus, center, and inertia are always addressed by a good jump coach. Whether using a saddle or not, the focal cues and physical reinforcements are the same.

Start by laying a single rail flat on the ground. From the ground, lead your horse over the rail several times. Next, get on your horse and walk, trot, and canter over the ground rail. In the canter, and possibly in the trot, your horse may give a little jump over the rail so grab a handful of mane as you approach the rail. Practice a few times with the rail on the ground before raising it.

Raise the rail no more than six inches, and lead your horse over it several times at the walk, from the ground as before, then mount and walk, trot, and canter over the rail several times. Your horse may continue stepping over the rail more often than jumping it, but these exercises will give him a sense of comfort about jumping. When you raise the rail the next time (just one notch), he will have to jump it, but by then, he will regard the rail without suspicion.

There are several important concepts to understand at this point. The first is confidence. As the itancan, you must be confident that what you are leading your horse to do is within his capabilities, and you must show no focal or physical signs of doubt. Some riders approach jumps in a very defensive position, clamping their legs, bracing themselves, or moving their feet forward in front of the girth in case of a stop or runout. The horse feels this hesitation or expectation of trouble and begins to worry. The old saying

Many people are amazed that my horse Kola climbs stairs and rides in elevators. These are not tricks that I've taught him. He does all these things because I never gave any reason for him to believe that he couldn't. The first set of stairs that we ever encountered was treated no differently than a grassy hill. I held his lead, did not change my pace, did not look back to see if he could make it, and simply walked up. I knew that these stairs provided good footing before I approached them with Kola. Because the itancan did not hesitate, neither did the rest of the "herd." Walking into our first elevator was like walking into a box stall. He has also developed, on his own, a fondness for jumping onto stages, some as high as four feet. I think it's because he's the biggest ham I know!

The point is that if there is hesitation in the mind or body language of the itancan, the herd will act accordingly.

"hope for the best and prepare for the worst" has no place in Relationship Training. Remember, you are leading your horse. You must know before you make the request that your horse will do what you're asking, and if your relationship with your horse has been cultivated carefully based on clear communication and previous successes, he should not hesitate.

The focus required for jumping is different from that required for any other maneuver. To go over a jump, visualize the arc you will be taking. If you focus on the rail in front of you, so will your horse. If you focus on your line of travel, your horse will seek a straight line through the rail rather than over it, and simply incorporate it as a stride in his line of travel. Envision an arc going from your takeoff point over the rail to your landing point. If your focal cues say "over the jump" but you're hanging on for dear life, you are not ready to jump. Doing so will create a lack of trust between you and your horse.

Horses do a lot of communicating with their bodies. After interacting with a horse for a short amount of time, you can learn to understand his subtle body movements and language. Some basic body cues to watch for can be found in a horse's ears, eyes, and head.

Ears point to whatever the horse is focusing on, although a horse may devote only one ear to something that does not require his complete attention. Eyes convey moods or attitudes, much the same way that human eyes do. Raised eyebrows are a sign of apprehension or surprise, but creased, raised eyebrows signal fear or pain. Soft, relaxed eyes mean the horse understands or is content. Head level usually conveys the horse's readiness to get out of a situation (flee) or fight. For example, a raised head with sharply creased eyebrows is what you see just before a horse rears or turns to get away from his handler. A low head with straight neck is a warning (also ears are pinned).

Horses manifest their personalities during training. Kola's cycle of learning goes like this. At first, he's playful, not really concerned with training, he's just enjoying the change of scenery. Then

(continued at right)

EXERCISE TEN

. . . .

The Obstacle Course

ONCE YOU ARE PERFORMING MOUNTED EXERCISES CONFIDENTLY AND consistently with your horse, it's helpful to close your training sessions with a mini obstacle course. Set up a course of varied maneuvers—turns, stops, jumps or ground rails, circles, changes of direction, cone slaloms, etc. Establish the order of the course before mounting your horse; if you don't know the order of the maneuvers, your horse will not receive the confidence he needs from the itancan. Outdoor courses can be much more challenging than ring courses (although any type of course is helpful). Mother Earth provides more interesting props than barrels, PVC rails, and orange cones, so from time to time, go through this exercise on a trail to keep it fun and interesting.

Keep in mind that this exercise is supposed to be fun and creative. This is not a we-have-to-learn-this situation, so do not place the same demands on your horse as you would in intense training. Do not change the techniques for each maneuver, but approach this exercise with a lighter attitude.

Take your horse to the outside edge of the course and back to the start. Do not walk him through the middle of the course area, as he may become confused by this. Go through the course, allowing your horse to make decisions and figure things out as he relies on your cues to guide him. Have fun, and when you feel that your goal has been accomplished, your session is done. This exercise is a good way to end every training session on a fun note, giving your horse some practical application for the lessons he's learned. Creativity and imagination are what keeps your horse from getting bored while training.

Now that your horse has learned to understand your language, and you can better understand his, it is important not to fall into routines or ruts. Just as you pay attention to moments when your horse moves even the slightest bit forward, you must also be aware of the point where your horse says, "I've had enough." Most horses become bored very easily—ask any horse who cribs or paces. Be sensitive to signs that your horse finds a particular exercise boring: he may not execute the exercise completely, may become easily distracted, his head may hang. When you recognize your horse's signs of boredom, move on to something more challenging. Your horse will show you the amount of time you should spend on any one exercise. Do not, however, mistake a good bluff as a sign of exhaustion. Horses are not beyond manipulating their riders to get what they want, especially young horses. If your horse should try to manipulate you by balking, disobeying, or holding his breath—the equine equivalent of whining and pouting—ignore it. These bluffs will pass providing you do not acknowledge them in any fashion. Don't punish your horse for them, just quietly insist by continuing to ask your horse to perform the exercise.

comes apprehension. He acts as if to say, "Oh, I get it. This is one of those training sessions." After training for a while, he may deliberately begin to ignore me in hopes of quitting early. He may even "pout" a little by stomping. But if I insist quietly, he submits, much like a child who realizes that no matter how much he kicks and screams, he must clean his room before he goes out to play. After a while, Kola exhibits boredom by adopting a blank stare, hanging his lower lip, beginning to lower his head, and maybe drooling.

The better you know your horse, the more easily you will be able to tell the difference between a legitimate problem and an equine tantrum or manipulation. For example, if your horse tries to move toward something in particular when he's balking during a lesson—such as a field, pasturemates, the barn, or a gate—the behavior probably is manipulative. He's testing you to see if he really has to do the exercise, or if he can get you to give up so he can go back to grazing. On the other hand, if he is merely moving away from something with no apparent agenda, it is usually because of confusion or fear. Knowing your horse well will give you the skills to interpret his behavior.

Exercise Eleven

. . . .

Leksi! Leksi! [leh-K'SHEE leh-K'SHEE] —Uncle! Uncle!

THE LAKOTA LEGEND *LEKSI! LEKSI!* WAS TOLD TO YOUNG RIDERS BEFORE THEY practiced their focal abilities with horses. Young riders were told to take their horses out at night and maneuver them using only their focal cues. If at any time they felt frightened or confused, they could call out, *"Leksi! Leksi!"* and Walking Crow and Laughing Beaver would guide them home safely.

Training at night is a good activity for anyone who wants to strengthen a bond with a horse. A moonlit night can make this experience extra special. If you do not feel comfortable riding in the dark, however, don't do it. For you to ride your horse in the dark with a feeling of fear and confusion will damage rather than strengthen your trust-bond with him.

Practicing your focal abilities at night works best in open fields or pastures. Choose your riding area carefully and survey it during the daytime for gopher holes, rocks, wire or boards on the ground, debris, broken fences, and other hazards.

When you first attempt this exercise, choose a night with a full or near-full moon, low wind, and no cloud cover to obstruct the moon. Mount your horse in the field and allow a few moments for both of you to get accustomed to training at night. Horses are more comfortable in the dark than most humans, so most of the work to get comfort levels up will be focused on yourself. You may think that your horse will not respond as quickly as he did in the ring during the day, but you may be surprised at how consistently your riding cues are interpreted by him. After all, your cues thus far have not been visual, so why should nighttime compromise their clarity? However, the darkness does intensify the need for a strong focal connection between you and your horse, and that's why this exercise is a good one for building bonds.

The object of this exercise is to zigzag across and up and down the field, all the while reinforcing your horse's ability to decipher your focal cues. Focus on a spot somewhere in the field and adjust your combined enter accordingly, exactly as you would when training in a ring or arena during the day. You may need to reinforce your focus with subtle physical commands, but your horse should not have trouble grasping your focal cues if you have properly executed the exercises prior to this one. When you have come within ten to twenty yards of your original focal point, choose another. This exercise is a lot of fun and can be great when the heat of summer limits daytime riding.

LEKSI! LEKSI!

Lakota

One morning in winter, the sun failed to appear on the eastern horizon. A council meeting was held and the elders decided that a scouting party of four should ride to the east to find out what had happened and to evaluate the situation. One of the scouts, Walking Crow, thought that because the sun had last been seen on the western horizon, it must still be hiding there, so he rode west. The other three scouts returned ten days later, having found no answers. Walking Crow did not return after ten days. He did not return after twenty days, and he did not return after thirty days. Still, the sky was dark.

Laughing Beaver, Walking Crow's nephew, became concerned about his Uncle. Laughing Beaver's father had been killed in a skirmish, and Walking Crow had taken him in as his own son. After thirty days of darkness, Laughing Beaver decided he would look for his uncle. He gathered his things, mounted his pony, and rode to the west.

The rest of the village held daily prayer councils and sweats in hopes of bringing back the sun. After a while, Walking Crow and Laughing Beaver were counted among the dead. They were not spoken of in the village. Then, after three years of darkness, the sun returned in the east as it had always done. The people were happy and the elders held a special ceremony thanking Creator. The ceremony was held at the eastern-most part of the people's range in honor of the sun's return to the east. During the prayers, a young boy pointed out two strange creatures grazing in the valley below. They appeared to be ponies with scouts on their backs, but the scouts had no legs. They seemed to be attached to the ponies' backs. The medicine man, Big Tree, said that those two strange creatures were Walking Crow and Laughing Beaver and their ponies, and that because the two scouts had spent three years on their ponies' backs in the darkness, they and their ponies had become one. Big Tree also said that Walking Crow and Laughing Beaver must have chased the sun all the way from the west to the east, and that their names should remain in the people's hearts always.

Kaonspe [kah-OON-spay]
Teaching with Force

There will be times in your training when your horse tests your status as itancan. It is only natural for your horse to do this and there is only one correct way to regain your status, assuming that your horse is an adult. Disobedience and aggression should be dealt with by a clear, abrupt message that says, "This behavior will not be tolerated!"

In a herd, the itancan continually reasserts his position in order to retain it. This is done with a swift kick or a sharp bite. Once is usually enough to thwart a challenger's efforts, then life in the herd returns to normal. Too often, horse owners yell and scream, kicking and hitting their horses, and throw fits when their horses follow a natural instinct to challenge the itancan and move up in status within the herd. You must deal with disobedience and challenges in the same way that the itancan horse would deal with them.

It's important to recognize the difference between a horse's attempts to move up the hierarchy within a two-member herd and a sign of aggression with intent to harm. A slow, steady pull of the head as a sign of resistance by your horse should be reprimanded with a correction in the opposite direction, either with a slow steady pull or a series of quick tugs.

A bite is a sign of aggression and dominance and should be dealt with by matching or exceeding the amount and type of aggression displayed by your horse. A sharp slap to the chest, accompanied by a short, loud yell, is usually enough to reestablish dominance. Kicking is also a sign of aggression, but is not as severe as one might think; a good kick can be very painful to two-leggeds, but in the herd situation, it is usually nothing more than a mild reprimand. Although you should not tolerate kicking, do not treat kicking in the same way as you would biting, because it might provoke another kick from your horse. Try raising the offending leg in the same manner you would use to pick up the hoof and hold for a few minutes. This mildly uncomfortable position is usually enough to get the message across.

Bucking is more often than not a response to fear or pain. One of the worst things you can do to a horse who bucks is jump off and yell at or physically reprimand him. Either of these responses only reinforces the fear or pain that caused the behavior.

Experienced trainers should handle the task of correcting or adjusting a horse's attitude, but in many cases if you understand your horse's motivations, you can correct these problems before they become dangerous. Nine out of ten times, these behaviors can be changed by returning to basic, relationship-building exercises.

Longeing Alternatives

The art of longeing, in its purest form, is an excellent method for training horses to respond to our communications. Done correctly, longeing is nothing less than beautiful. It is truly an art form and can take many years to master. Originally, longeing was used as a way of training a horse to respond to verbal and physical cues while on the ground. Unfortunately, in many cases longeing has deteriorated into a mindless exercise wherein a horse who is tied to a rope runs in a circle around a whip-wielding trainer. The following are alternatives to mindless longeing and will strengthen, rather than weaken, the relationship that you are developing with your horse.

Warming Up

In the limited spaces found at most horse shows, ride your horse in that circle you might otherwise have longed him in. This provides you with ability to exercise your horse, exercise yourself, reinforce your relationship, and stretch and warm up tight muscles.

Bit Training

Teaching a young horse to respond to the bit can be done using a tool developed by the Nez Percé called *akita mani yo* (ah-KEE-tah MAH-nee yo) by the Lakota. Fit the *akita mani yo*, or surcingle, behind your horse's withers and tighten the girth just enough to keep it in place. Tie a fourteen foot length of rope to each side of the bit and run the ropes through the rings on either side of the *akita mani yo*. Make sure the rope is not so thick that it cannot slide through the rings freely.

From the ground, face your horse with one rein of rope in each hand. If you are holding the ends of the reins, you should be about seven or eight feet in front of your horse. Lead your horse by walking backward, using the reins to reinforce your movements. Remember that pulling on the reins in this position will pull back on the horse's mouth. Focus your eyes on your horse's eyes and begin to walk through some simple maneuvers, all the while reinforcing your movements with slight pressure on the appropriate side of his mouth. As soon as you get a response from your horse, release the tension and reward your horse immediately.

By starting a young horse with the hakamya upo (come, follow closely) shadowing exercises, this exercise should be quite easy for your horse to accept and comprehend. When both you and your horse are comfortable with this exercise, you can turn around and walk forward rather than backward. I have found that horses are much more responsive to this method than they are to hooking a longe line to one side of the bit and using a longe whip to make them run around in a circle.

Cavaletti Work

Many trainers longe horses over cavaletti (a series of poles placed in the ground) to teach the horse to change leads, learn balance, gather himself, and engage his hind end. But it is usually much more effective to have some weight on the horse's back when doing cavaletti work. Not only can you communicate, build the relationship, and reinforce focal cues from your horse's back, but the added weight causes the horse to place his feet more carefully. If the horse should balk at first, do not tell him to disregard his apprehension and run through it anyway. Dismount and lead him through the cavaletti at a walk, trot, and canter. You'll be surprised at how easy he then goes over them with you remounted. Remember, lead by example.

Jumping

Longeing a horse over jumps frequently causes serious accidents. The combination of an airborne horse, a thirty-foot longe line, and lightweight wooden poles and jump standards does not make for a safe training environment. If you are trying to teach your horse to take off and land correctly, ride your horse over mock jumps—poles on the ground. If you are trying to teach your horse to become comfortable with jumps, lead him through them. Remember, if you think you're teaching your horse to jump, you're mistaken; he already knows how.

Reprimand

It is common to see a rider attempting to bore his horse to death by running the horse around in a circle at the end of a longe line. This method of reprimand goes against everything in this book and 99 percent of the time ends up with nothing more than a tired, bored horse. If a horse misbehaves during a training session, deal with the infraction then. If he shows aggression toward you, respond immediately and unmistakably. Your horse will not connect longeing with his misbehavior by the time you've dismounted, fetched your longe line and whip, perhaps untacked him, and led him to the longeing area.

Submission

Unruly horses are sometimes put on the end of a longe line and made to run around in circles until they grow tired and are forced to submit to the trainer. The stud chain is usually affixed over the nose so that the trainer can tug on it for the purposes of reprimand. This exercise does not a relationship make. I think that those who employ this practice should be given the opportunity to train lions or tigers once or twice.

Time, Patience, and Consistency

There is no substitute for spending time with an animal when trying to build a relationship. It is not necessary to spend a lot of time with your horse, but the time spent must be time devoted to just you and your horse. None of us is able to spend as much time with our horses as we would like, but it is not the quantity of time that builds healthy working relationships, but rather the quality of that time. Remember, if you are not teaching your horse good habits at any given time, then he is learning bad ones. If you have a sincere desire to build a relationship with your horse, your actions will reflect it. If, on the other hand, a better relationship sounds like a good idea, but you are content with what works now, the time will elude you. Many of the exercises in this book require no more than thirty minutes, but they must be thirty minutes of undivided attention and commitment to building the relationship.

Put simply, you will reap what you sow. If you are in a boarding situation, set aside one or two times a week when you can give your horse a half hour of your undivided attention. Even the most basic exercises in this book are designed to build relationships, and a half hour of solid concentration and commitment can be just as strenuous as a three- or four-hour trail ride. If you can spend only ten minutes a week working on an exercise that strengthens your relationship with your horse, make that ten minutes prosperous by dedicating your efforts entirely. The results you reap from ten minutes of a focused relationship exercise equals or exceeds the results gained in a month by the majority of horse owners using modern horse training methods. Remember, quality not quantity.

Waonspekiye, (wah-OON-spay-KEE-yay), or teaching with patience, means treating your horse the same way that you would a child who has difficulty learning or grasping new concepts. If you afford your horse the same understanding, concern, and patience, you will reap amazing results. Many of the same techniques and exercises that Relationship Training incorporates for use with horses are used in special education classes to teach learning-disabled students. These are methods such as giving immediate rewards, taking many small steps rather than a few large ones to teach a concept, and basing each lesson on the achievement of the previous lesson. Patience is what determines whether a particular horse will become a champion or a horse for sale.

The object of any exercise is not to teach a horse how to do something; most of what a rider needs a horse to do are things the horse already knows how to do. The object is to teach a horse how to understand your form of communication so he will respond appropriately to your requests. This can be laborious. Your horse will grasp certain concepts faster than others. Can you remember learning an entirely new concept in high school, perhaps a physics formula or algebra? For most of us, there was a point at which we said, "Oh, I get it." It is much the same for horses.

I remember one horse in particular who seemed as dumb as a bag of doorknobs when it came to switching leads. I worked with this animal for six weeks, and still the horse would go blank anytime we tried the lead changing exercises. At liberty, however, she changed leads just as naturally as she drank water.

Then, one day it happened. While working on strengthening her ability to interpret physical commands in a figure eight pattern, she changed her leads correctly over and over again. I rewarded her immediately and generously and got successful lead changes thereafter. When I got off her back and gave her a big hug, she gave me a look as if to say, "If that was all you wanted me to do, why didn't you say so?" As usual, it was the human's inability to communicate— not the horse's inability to perform a task—that had this particular trainer pulling his hair out. Although for some trainers it is very hard to develop, when it comes to interacting with horses, patience is not only a virtue, but a necessary quality.

E li quu [el-EE-koo-oo]
ENOUGH

No encyclopedia of horsemanship ever existed among this continent's first great horsemen. Because of the great diversity found among the tribes that inhabited North America, it would not have been possible two hundred years ago to collect and organize their methods and approaches.

The ideas and exercises in this book are the things that I have learned from the elders of different Nations. I have had the wonderful opportunity of traveling around this country, speaking and performing on weekends at powwows and cultural festivals. During the week, I learned as much as the elders of that local tribe could teach me about horsemanship. I was raised alongside horses, and while on the road (if I did not have my horse with me), found it hard to stay away from them. I discovered that no matter what part of the country I was in, a stable owner or friend on the reservation could always direct me to the local "Indian authority on horses."

We have reason to glory in the achievements of our ancestors.

—O no'sa

It is to these authorities that I owe much of my knowledge of the old ways concerning horses. It is for them that I attempt to record their methods here. I do not claim to know all of the answers, but I do claim to know a few. Most of the answers I know are to the questions concerning relationships. It is extremely important to establish a healthy working relationship with your horse before attempting to produce results.

You must first establish yourself as itancan. When your horse accepts you as itancan you must then reinforce your position on a regular, or routine, basis. You must be consistent with every new exercise. Do not attempt any exercise in which your ability to lead is inferior to your horse's. If you lack the confidence to do something, do not ask your horse to follow.

I hope that this book has planted a few seeds of awareness and inspiration, and that the exercises contained herein are helpful to you. I will continue to learn from the elders for as long as Creator sees fit and will pass on to you the knowledge of this nation's first great horsemen.

The exercises in this book are fairly simple and focus on basics because it is difficult to learn consistency when working on exercises that you are not very comfortable with. It is much easier to consistently work on stop and go than it is to consistently work on spin around and lie down. Don't move on from the basics until your training techniques are consistent enough to warrant more complicated exercises. If you do things differently every time you work with your horse, even on very small things, you will send mixed messages to him and communication will become ineffective. Consistency is paramount when working with your horse. Without it, you will get nowhere.

I feel
glad
as the ponies do
when the
fresh green grass starts
in the
beginning of

PARTING WORDS

Our paths crossing is not a mistake. Though our Grandmothers could not know which flowers we would pick or which stones would make us stumble, our Creator surely did. Creator knew of the tree that would provide shade and the lake that would wet hair. Creator knew of the dog that would lick our face.

I am young and do not know many things, but this I know—our paths crossing is not a mistake. It took many wars and much bloodshed so that we might meet. Our Grandmothers and their Grandmothers bore much pain, shed many tears, and called out to their children in the forest many times so that our paths might cross. Our Grandfathers walked many miles, so many miles. They prayed and they dreamed so that we might meet. The turkeys called in the spring, and the crows danced on the fall winds so that we might speak. The people pushed on, even though they were cold and hungry, so that we might be together. They knew not who we were, yet they moved forward for our benefit. And the little people did their jobs well. They placed the sticks and stones and feathers where they were supposed to so that we might pick them up, so that we might think and pray and dream.

And so now, after many years and many Grandmothers and many wars, we meet. And you ask, "Who are you?" I am your brother. The one that your Grandmothers died for and for whom many wars were fought. I am the one that was led to you by so many sticks, stones, and feathers. I am the one who will walk and cry and pray and fight so that they might meet.

The year.

—Ten Bears

And still you ask, "Who are you? You are a stranger to me." I am the one who was born and raised and brought up by my parents so that our paths might cross. I am the one who learned to fish and hunt and who cried at my sister's burial so that we might speak. But still you do not recognize me. Perhaps I am wrong. Perhaps they were wrong. Perhaps we should not smile or say hello while passing. Perhaps all those wars and prayers and dreams and tears were not so that we might meet.

But my Grandparents spoke of you and they were honorable people. They would not waste all of those wars and prayers and dreams and tears if we were not meant to meet. They did not know which flowers we would pick or which stones would make us stumble, but they knew that our paths would cross. I am young and do not know many things but this I know— our paths crossing is not a mistake.

The stones do not always recognize the water rushing over them, but they know that it is not a mistake. Our paths have crossed for a reason, a reason Creator knows of. We must now find out why, and in doing so, ensure that their paths will also cross. This I know.

SELECTED BIBLIOGRAPHY

Bowker, Nancy and Eustis-Cross, Barbara. *The Wild Horse, an Adopter's Manual.* New York: Howell Book House, 1992.

Caduto, Michael J.; Bruchac, Joseph. *Keepers of the Earth.* Golden: Fulcrum Publishing, 1988-89.

Clairborne, Robert. *The First Americans.* New York: Time-Life Books, 1973.

Clark, La Verne Harrell. *They Sang for Horses, The Impact of the Horse on Navajo and Apache Folklore.* Arizona: University of Arizona Press, 1966.

Hoxie, Frederick E., editor. *Encyclopedia of North American Indians.* Boston and New York: Houghton Mifflin Company, 1996.

Johnson, Sandy (as told to). *The Book of Elders.* San Francisco: HarperSanFrancisco, HarperCollins Publishers, 1994.

Jurmain, Suzanne. *Once Upon a Horse.* New York: Lothrop, Lee & Shepard Books, 1989.

Maxwell, James A. *American's Fascinating Indian Heritage.* Pleasantville, New York and Montreal, The Reader's Digest Association, Inc., 1978.

Mooney, Michael MacDonald, editor. *George Catlin Letters and Notes on the North American Indians.* New York: Clarkson N. Potter, Inc., 1975.

Ortiz, Alfonso, Volume 9 Editor. *The Handbook of North American Indians Southwest.* Washington: Smithsonian Institution, 1979.

Preston, Douglas. *Cities of Gold.* New York: Simon & Schuster, 1993.

Taylor, Louis. *Bits: Their History, Use & Misuse.* North Hollywood: Wilshire Book Company, 1981.

Viola, Herman J. *After Columbus: The Smithsonian Chronicle of the North American Indians.* Washington: Smithsonian Books, 1993.

Welch, James; Stekler, Paul. *Killing Custer.* New York: W.W. Norton & Company, Inc., 1994.